MOSCOW

A guide to Soviet and post-Soviet architecture

...

Maria Kiernan
Photographs by Keith Collie

Moscow

A guide to Soviet and post-Soviet architecture

••• ellipsis KÖNEMANN

•••

CREATED, EDITED AND DESIGNED BY
Ellipsis London Limited
2 Rufus Street London N1 6PE
E MAIL ...@ellipsis.co.uk
www http://www.ellipsis.com
SERIES EDITOR Tom Neville
EDITOR Annie Bridges
SERIES DESIGN Jonathan Moberly
LAYOUT Pauline Harrison
PICTURES on pages 35 59, and 299
reproduced by kind permission of Yuri
Sdobnov

COPYRIGHT © 1998 Könemann
Verlagsgesellschaft mbH
Bonner Str. 126, D-50968 Köln
PRODUCTION MANAGER Detlev Schaper
PRINTING AND BINDING Sing Cheong
Printing Ltd
Printed in Hong Kong

ISBN 3 8290 0474 5 (Könemann)
ISBN 1 899858 59 8 (Ellipsis)

Maria Kiernan 1998

Contents

Introduction

Moscow, a vast city with a population in the region of 10 million and covering an area of over 800 square kilometres, may be described both geographically and culturally as the metropolis where East meets West. Situated on the eastern edge of Europe, it is the capital of a huge land mass, much of which is within the continent of Asia. The acceptance of Byzantine civilisation and the influx of Western values under Peter the Great were two important events in the development of Russian culture. These factors, together with location, play an important role in our understanding of the Russian people, whose unique qualities are a rich blend of these two diverse cultures. Moscow reflects the enigma and ambiguities of these passionate, sentimental and tolerant people who, at great cost and sacrifice to themselves, have shaped this built environment.

In architecture we find an enduring record of history: buildings, streets and town planning inform us of a way of life. Through this visual record we can interpret the needs, aspirations and values of a society. This guide attempts to give the reader a flavour of the recent architectural activity of this distinctive capital over a period that includes two sharp turns in Moscow's history. My selection – a personal choice – begins more than 75 years ago in the early idealistic days of the Soviet Union, and concludes with the turbulent decade which followed the collapse of Communism, and the formative years of the market economy which replaced it.

History has seen this great city destroyed and rebuilt several times, which is one reason for Muscovites' pride in conserving and at times reinstating their historical environment. Moscow's development began in the 12th century as a minor principality on an intersection of trade routes between Slavonic states. A fortified Kremlin marked the foundation of the town in 1147, with its distinctive radial structure developing around this on the hills surrounding the Moskva river. In the 13th and 14th centuries the town suffered Mongolian invasions and was burned to the ground. On becoming the capital of Russia in the 15th century, the original Kremlin was reconstructed. Later, in the early 16th century, its timber ramparts were replaced by new stone fortifications. In 1703 Peter the Great moved the capital to his new, purpose-built St Petersburg. Eclipsed by the imperial capital, Moscow took an historical back seat until the collapse of Tsarism in 1917. During the intervening period there was further destruction: in 1812, 70 per cent of buildings were destroyed by fire as Muscovites burned their own city, successfully thwarting Napoleon's invading army. The reconstruction that rapidly followed included a number of new squares and the development of boulevards along the radial avenues.

After the October revolution, in March 1918 the Bolsheviks – concerned at the proximity of Petrograd (St Petersburg's new name) to western borders – moved the 'supreme organs of state power' to Moscow, establishing it as the capital of the new Soviet Union. During its difficult early years, the country – only recently devastated by the First World War – became enmeshed in a grim civil war.

Soviet architecture was born during this time of tremendous upheaval. Ambitious five-year plans were implemented with Herculean effort; most notably, Lenin's vision for the electrification of Russia was realised in less than the projected 15 years. Two early legislative acts within months of the revolution were of paramount importance: the socialisation of land and the repeal of rights to private ownership of property within the cities. As a direct result of the implementation of this legislation, social patterns in urban areas changed drastically. With municipal control over housing stock, space considered in excess of an individual's needs was taken over and redistributed. As the urban population increased, this process resolved the most acute housing shortages; by 1924 around half a million people were resettled in Moscow alone. New forms of community life were evolving, and architects responded enthusiastically in their first attempts to create new types of communes. An active search also began for a new language of architectural expression, opposing the old and familiar with something modern deliberately contradictory. Architectural opinions differed on how this should be achieved. Conservative academicians such as Zholtovsky, Fomin and Shchusev produced solutions which promulgated the historical style, using classical motifs, in sharp contrast to the innovative modern visions, which developed into two opposing trends. Rationalists, led by Ladovsky – in a relatively small group known as ASNOVA (Association of New Architects) – assumed spatial arrangement was the main objective of architecture, with aesthetics of structure and materials secondary; whereas constructivists, under the chairmanship of Alexander Vesnin – in an association known as OSA (Association of Contemporary Architects) – considered function and structure should dictate building form.

Following an important 1923 competition for the design of the Palace of Labour, the novel technical forms of the third-place entry by the Vesnin brothers received much acclaim, and paved the way for constructivism in architecture. Functionalism rather than aesthetics was seen as the main goal of this new means of building, with the machine and its 'total absence of idle elements' as its model. Constructivism was intended as a working method rather than a style. However, its success turned it at times into a fashionable and much imitated dressing on often mediocre compositions. Emanating from a new culture, constructivism is the sole movement in 20th-century Soviet architectural development that has contributed significantly to the history of world architecture.

The Workers' Club or Palace was a new building type which represented some of the best examples of this genre. Considered the heart of socialist culture, these buildings were required to be different in design from the general context of city construction. This inspired many leading architects – including the Vesnin brothers, Melnikov and others – to create their own individual aesthetic solutions during this exciting but short period of avant-garde architecture.

In the 1920s and '30s, the years of 'socialist industrialisation', there was a huge increase in Moscow's population – to 5 million. The main instrument of state for the rational organisation of Communist society was 'the Plan'; in urban design this took the form of 'the Master Plan', providing the blueprint for the development of the city in the subsequent five to 15 years. The first master plan of the city was adopted in 1935, following Stalin's brief to present Moscow as the showcase capital of 'the world's first socialist state'. Its wide streets, together with boulevards, bridges and embankments converging on a necklace of skyscrapers, dictated the framework for future development of the Soviet capital, including the demolition of streets and the district around the Kremlin.

A Party decree in 1932 – demanding the disbanding of all creative groups and their regrouping as centralised unions under Communist Party control – brought about the end of avant-garde design. During the following years of intense construction, architectural expression became monumental – to abnormal proportions – with scale and decoration tending towards the neo-classical. This ideology was made public in the brief for the competition to design the Palace of Soviets, which required the entrants to draw on 'the best examples of classical architecture'. The Party line was defined as social realism, and those not conforming to it were prevented from building: under Stalin's reign of terror some architects, including the constructivist leader Alexei Gan, were arrested and sent to die in labour camps. The most ambitious scheme during this period was the development of an underground public transport system, begun in 1931. Designers were instructed to create 'the best underground in the world', a symbol of 'the triumph of socialism'. The first of these spectacular stations – and instruments of Stalinist propaganda – opened in 1935.

Development of the city grew confidently and swiftly until interrupted in 1941 by the invasion of the German army and the Soviet Union's entry into the Second World War. Amazingly, construction continued during the war years, albeit mainly on industrial projects in the east. Even so, the amount of new building surpassed the volume of the pre-war five-year plans, and in Moscow work continued on the underground.

Following the horrendous devastation of the war years – more than 26 million Soviets had been killed, and one third of the USSR's wealth destroyed – reconstruction and restoration became a historical task of the utmost importance. Cultural values and heritage assumed a special significance, with increased symbolism and the embellishment of monumental Stalinist classicism. The victorious triumphalism and nationalism found in the architecture of the post-war period was focused on public buildings, as reflected in the decision to build a system of high-rise landmark buildings, the reconstruction of the All Union Agricultural Exhibition (page 216), and the continuing development of the metro. All were designed with the intention of changing the image of the capital and marking the beginning of 'a superior period of Socialist architecture'. An enormous amount of money was lavished on these monumental constructions – often on expensive decorative finishes –

at a time of great need, with most of the city's population living in cramped, communal apartments.

After the 20th Congress in 1956, and Khrushchev's famous speech denouncing Stalin, a programme was published to democratise Soviet society. By the end of the 1950s Khrushchev's radical reforms saw a new technically-driven period in architecture, where rationalist attitudes and social objectives prevailed. The practice of 'architectural excess' in building and planning was condemned, with individualised projects replaced by standardised construction using a limited number of prototype designs. Quick, inexpensive, precast solutions resulted. This attempt to alleviate housing shortages created residential districts on the outskirts of the city where quantity rather than quality was the order of the day.

The early 1960s saw a quest for a new means of expression. The Palace of Congresses (see page 24), built in 1961, became the new model for public buildings: its architects, part of a small group, were responsible for all public representative structures over the next decade. However, the Palace of Young Pioneers (page 252), with its asymmetrical plan in the middle of a green site – and a polemic far removed from the sterile monumentality of the previous era – marked the beginning of a new direction in architecture.

The 1970s and '80s under Brezhnev saw for the most part faceless mass construction, and is referred to as the period of stagnation. Economic and political direction at this time was aimed at maintaining the status quo; culturally it was a period of conservatism and increased censorship. The 1970s did not produce any single stylistic trend; public buildings during this period are diverse, characterised by a revival of interest in national traditions. A search continued for new construction methods for residential development, with blocks becoming higher and denser over the decade. At the same time there was a preoccupation with the most effective use of land and the spatial patterns between individual blocks. In contrast, places of public entertainment such as theatres and circuses used monumental and decorative art to produce a lively imagery and some of the most romantic creations of this otherwise dull period.

The brightest manifestation of the early 1980s was 'Paper Architecture', a movement formed by young conceptual architects involved primarily in competitions. Their success on the world stage gave fresh impetus to the movement, which spread rapidly. Although producing stunning drawings representing a fantastical vision of a complex imaginary city, they rarely offered tangible solutions for urban improvement.

In 1986 Gorbachev as Communist Party leader initiated a three-part programme that was expected to herald a golden age of Soviet design. *Perestroika* (restructuring), *glasnost* (openness), and democratisation were intended as tools to make the Soviet regime more human and more productive, but in reality events took a very different course. Instability spread throughout the Soviet Union, causing economic crisis – manifest in inflation and shortages of even the most basic goods – and undermining any serious design efforts among emerging private enterprises.

Following the collapse of the Soviet Union in 1991, new and radically different social, economic and political structures are being established. This difficult process, still under way, has accelerated greatly in the second half of the 1990s. Construction, slow in the initial years, has escalated dramatically – initially with foreign investment, and subsequently with Russian. Strong activity in the building sector combined with a tenacious mayor has revitalised the city, with many parts of the centre restored in time for its 850th anniversary in 1997. But one feels that opportunities are being missed, as architects – following the dictate of the municipality

– resort to pastiche when restoring or 'reinstating' buildings, with no calibration of their previous merit.

New building types include banks, hotels, commercial and office developments. Once Russian architects became free to experiment and explore recent trends, Western influences and new styles became evident – led by post-modernism. 'Volume and spatial composition' are principles that dominate the Moscow architect's perception, sometimes to the exclusion of the more subtle but important balancing elements such as texture and colour.

There has been much discussion in the architectural profession about a 'New Moscow style', a phenomenon whose existence is not substantiated in the majority of cases. A popular feature of these invariably postmodernly dressed structures is an obligatory vertical element – usually a tower pushing up from one extremity of the façade – a solution that would seem to be encouraged by the municipality. This said, there are a number of recent developments whose 'soul' is clearly Russian, their design emanating from the eclectic patchwork of styles that is Moscow.

Recent achievements in architecture must be appreciated in the context of the internal political and bureaucratic struggles that complicate their design and construction. The level of the authorities' interference in an architect's sphere of competence – that of design – is most clearly manifested in the disastrous Manezh shopping complex (see page 38). For even the most talented of the private practices that have started up in recent years, gaining commissions has been difficult. Massive state architectural offices – known as Mosproekts – remain, and with their long-established and close associations with the authorities, they directly or through associated private studios enjoy the lion's share of the market.

Building project organisation – from conception through the procurement process to completion – has not changed since Soviet times. Though the profession has assisted in educating its members on new procedures, it is still struggling tirelessly to have this process regulated and brought into the 1990s.

ACKNOWLEDGEMENTS
Thank you to: Jonathan and Tom, for inviting me to be a part of this terrific series and providing me with a plausible excuse to spend more time in a city I have come to consider my second home; Keith, for letting me share his fresh enthusiasm at discovering for himself this magical city, reflected in his excellent photographs; Paul, for being there when I wasn't, for proof reading and for encouragement; Olga Artemova, for patient and endless assistance in translating and checking the transliteration; Yuri Petrovich and Elena Andreevna, for love and support; Yuri Afanasyevich, for his humour and much more. Also I would like to extend my gratitude to The Union of Architects of Russia; the Russian Embassy in Ireland; the Irish Trade Board; Serge Merzhanov; Yuri Volchok; Svetlana and Igor Gaverilov; Svetlana and Igor Pissarsky; Olga Shcherbakova; and to Gress Kiernan, for all those thankless tasks that only a mother would undertake.
MK February 1998

Moscow: a guide to Soviet and post-Soviet architecture

Using this book

The names of buildings and locations are those in use at the time of writing; where they have superseded previous Soviet names these are also included in the text. All names are transliterated into Roman script. Numbering of floors is generally in accordance with the Russian system, with the first floor corresponding to the European ground floor.

Access to most buildings is controlled. In a habit left over from Soviet days, entrances are generally guarded by individuals who take their position seriously, appearing to believe the old regime is still in place. Behind their crusty masks often lurk kind souls, and you can be lucky. But be warned – if you do get in you may be disappointed by the sad state of many of the interiors. However, with official buildings of any sort, forget it – in some cases even photographing the exterior is not permitted.

All the buildings selected are within the outer city ring road and are within walking distance of a metro station. Though Moscow is a large city, distances are comfortably covered – except in rush hours – in the efficient underground. In fact the journey through this stunning subterranean world can form an enjoyable and stimulating part of the excursion. The metro operates from 06.00 until 01.00, with trains as frequent as every minute at peak times. Signposting is minimal and only in Cyrillic, which can be confusing, particularly if you have to change lines. Multijourney tickets or plastic tokens can be bought in the entrance vestibules of all stations.

Other forms of public transport include trolley buses and trams, but if you do not have a knowledge of the language the metro is simpler to negotiate. Taxis are not recommended unless absolutely necessary. Traffic jams can now be encountered at all times of the day and night, due to a massive increase of cars on the road, largely of the luxury imported variety.

The guide is divided into nine sections. The first three follow the radial roads and the area around the historic nucleus of the Kremlin, and are largely negotiable on foot – although during the winter months it is probably best to use the metro. Beyond the inner ring roads the city is too sprawling and transport will be needed. The last section is dedicated to the metro itself, with the stations listed chronologically.

Names found in the addresses include:

BOLSHOY/BOLSHAYA big
BULVAR boulevard
MALY/MALAYA small
MOST bridge
NABEREZHNAY embankment
NOVY/NOVAYA new
PEREULOK lane
PROSPEKT avenue
PLOSHCHAD square
PROEZD entrance
SAD garden
SHOSSE highway
STARY/STARAYA OLD
ULITSA street

Moscow: a guide to Soviet and post-Soviet architecture

Around the Kremlin

Lenin Mausoleum

In January 1924, immediately after the death of Vladimir Ilyich Lenin, a modest timber mausoleum was hastily erected in Red Square to house his remains and to allow the Soviet people to pay their respects. This simple low grey cube with a stepped roof and pyramidal volume was positioned below the Kremlin Wall, close to where the revolutionary casualties of 1917 were buried. Its siting was also determined by the square's transverse axis, from the cupola of the Council of Ministers to the Senate Tower.

The request of Lenin's family that he be buried was ignored, and by spring 1924 the original building had been replaced with a larger, more imposing timber structure. Following the same principles as its predecessor, it was also intended as a temporary monument while decisions were made as how best to perpetuate Lenin's memory.

The final design was completed in 1930, concurrent with the rebuilding of Red Square. This included constructing reviewing stands on either side of the mausoleum, knocking down old buildings at the river end of the square, and moving the Minin and Pozharsky Monument from the centre of the square (had it remained, the figures of the two heroes would have been pointing aggressively towards the mausoleum). On Stalin's death in 1953 his remains briefly joined Lenin's in the mausoleum, but were moved to the Kremlin Wall after Khrushchev's famous speech denouncing Stalin at the 20th Congress.

This monumental building with its combined historicism and avant-garde approach has played a large part in the development of Soviet architecture, particularly in the context of continuity in the development of historic cities. Experimentation with the timber structures helped Shchusev achieve the beautifully proportioned form of the final stone-dressed concrete building. The decision to combine the memorial building

A V Shchusev 1924–30

A V Shchusev 1924–30

with a stand from which Soviet leaders could watch parades also helped to make the building bigger than the earlier models. With great skill, Shchusev created a superb contemporary building whose relatively modest size belies its compositional influence over the entire square. With its rich red and black polished stone, the crisp, modern, undecorated ensemble is in harmony with the Kremlin walls behind, yet maintains a strong individual identity.

A visit to the mausoleum and Lenin's embalmed remains was for decades part of many visitors' itinerary. After long queues and much security, one proceeded respectfully towards the central doors, descended a staircase and entered the main chamber at Lenin's right shoulder. Walking around the perimeter of the room, one silently viewed the suited remains laid on a tilted slab before exiting on the right-hand side. The procession then continued to the cemetery behind, where many Soviet leaders are buried or their ashes interred in urns set in the Kremlin Wall.

Following the 1991 coup and the subsequent break-up of the Soviet Union, there has been much talk about the fate of Lenin's body. The ceremonial changing of the guards ceased and the mausoleum doors were temporarily closed to visitors. Alternative proposals were prepared for the total redesign of Red Square, many of which included demolition of the mausoleum. But as time passed, the folly of obliterating an important part of Russia's heritage became apparent. Although again on view to visitors, in the not-too-distant future Lenin's remains are likely to be removed and finally interred.

ADDRESS Red Square
METRO Ploshchad Revolutsii

A V Shchusev 1924–30

A V Shchusev 1924–30

Palace of Congresses

Just inside the Trinity Tower entrance to the Kremlin is Senate Square, on the left of which stand both the Arsenal and Senate buildings. After the 1917 revolution the 18th-century Senate was used by the Soviet Government – Lenin's office and apartment were located here. On the opposite side of the square the stark modern intervention of the Kremlin Palace of Congresses disrupts the harmony of this sensitive historical setting. The result of an architectural competition initiated under Khrushchev in 1959, the building was officially opened in 1961. Although the palace was controversial, those who commissioned it considered it such a success that the architects were awarded a Lenin Prize in 1962, and it set the trend for the architecture of the 1960s. A few years later Mikhail Posokhin and Ashot Mndoyants were also the leading architects responsible for the development of Kalinin Prospekt (now called Novy Arbat, see page 76).

To reduce its visual impact beyond the Kremlin walls and to keep its height within that of adjacent structures, the building level starts 15 metres below ground. This solution has been very successful – viewing the Kremlin from across the river or from the main bridge, the modern structure is completely masked by earlier buildings.

Fins from ground to cornice level divide the full-height glazing. The strong vertical emphasis this creates, combined with the severe white marble cladding of the concrete structure, contrasts sharply with its richly rendered period neighbours. Above the cut-stone cornice, the top floor of the banqueting hall is set back, crowning the building with an incongruous rhythm of glazing.

Internally the building is more successful. Intended for congresses of the Supreme Soviet of the Communist Party and other important gatherings, it was also (and still is) a venue for theatrical and concert perform-

Various architects 1959–61

Various architects 1959–61

ances. The virtually uninterrupted glazing to the front and sides of the spacious foyer and upper landings provides an excellent panorama of the landscape beyond. The view, disturbed only by a mesh of stairs and escalators, is particularly enchanting in winter. The sizeable places of assembly function extremely well, effortlessly disseminating the thousands who gather for each performance by means of wide curved stairs which link the main auditorium above and the cloakroom below.

Worth a visit at the lower level below the central stairs are the men's toilets. Their curved walls and sheer size, magnified by mirrors, produce a remarkable effect – or so it seemed on my brief accidental encounter. The women's facilities are far less numerous and only of practical interest.

The main auditorium, with softly raked amphitheatre and balcony above, seats almost 6000 people. The configuration of the hall and the selection of finishes provide excellent acoustics. Because of the level of technical equipment installed, the auditorium also has considerable flexibility, making it possible to stage many types of performance. The second-largest public area is the banqueting hall, an open space of more than 4000 square metres occupying the top floor of the building.

Around the Kremlin

ADDRESS Kremlin, Senate Square
ARCHITECTS M V Posokhin, A A Mndoyants, Y M Stamo, P P Shteller, N Shchepetilnikov, G Lvov, A Kondratyëv, I Kochetov
METRO Alexandrovsky Sad, Biblioteka Imeni Lenina

Various architects 1959–61

Various architects 1959–61

Lenin Library

Following competitions held between 1926 and 1929 for the design of the State Library of the USSR Lenin Library complex, the constructivists and the classicists were united in their criticism of the winning scheme. The constructivists considered it a return to the old traditions, while the classicists perceived it as a vulgar betrayal. In response to this criticism, Shchuko and Gelfreikh produced a revised design in an aesthetic closer to their constructivist colleagues.

The resulting complex successfully brings together the two diametrically opposing architectural approaches in a modern classical monumental building. At the same time it cleverly fulfils the brief's requirement that the design take into account the neighbouring historical monuments of the Manezh and the Kremlin, 'avoiding entering into flagrant contradiction with them'. At the design stage there was no sign of the classical elements of decoration that one sees on the finished building, and these have diluted the clarity of the original concept.

The library building is sited on the corner of Vozdvizhenka and Mokhovaya Ulitsy, on the foundations of the former library of neighbouring Pashkov House. In addition to storage for 36 million books, accommodation includes exhibition halls, auditoria, lecture rooms, concert halls, a book museum, administrative offices, reading rooms for 2300 people, and an entrance hall to the metro.

A large corner podium stepping down to both streets sets the main building back and separates it from the road. September 1997 saw a sculpture added to the podium. Set on a stone base, this larger-than-life seated figure represents a reading Dostoevsky.

The black granite columns of the main entrance portico support an entablature decorated with two levels of figures in relief, giving it further vertical emphasis and focus.

V A Shchuko, V G Gelfreikh 1928–41

V A Shchuko, V G Gelfreikh 1928–41

The building elevation has a very strong continuous vertical rhythm, which is picked up at the internal corner by elegant full-height square grey stone columns. These form a walkway wrapping around both the library building and the later book museum building, curtaining a courtyard leading to the latter. This sheltered colonnade was a popular meeting place in the pre-bar/restaurant days of the Soviet era.

From the main lobby a grand central staircase leads up to the brightly lit hall adjoining the reading areas. The grandeur continues through the interior, with marble floors and columns, coffered ceilings, and brass and bronze light fittings and balustrades.

ADDRESS Vozdvizhenka Ulitsa, 3
METRO Biblioteka Imeni Lenina

V A Shchuko, V G Gelfreikh 1928–41

V A Shchuko, V G Gelfreikh 1928–41

Moskva Hotel

The redesign of Red Square in the early 1930s was followed by the re-arrangement and widening of the streets surrounding the Kremlin. Small-scale structures were demolished, creating vast open spaces and large sites, one of which, around the former Okhotny Ryad (Hunter's Way), became the site of the hotel of Moscow City Council, now known as the Moskva Hotel.

This cumbersome building, with its heavy massing and laborious details, is considered a watershed in the development of Soviet architecture. It was designed and built at a time when Stalin was retreating from his brief patronage of constructivism towards the monumental classicism which was to dominate the next three decades. The hotel was one of the first key buildings in Stalin's reconstruction of Moscow, and its ponderous monumentality and strained pomposity became guidelines for the architecture of the 1930s.

As originally designed by Savelyev and Stapran, the hotel was a constructivist building with simple geometric volumes, light supports and smooth plain surfaces. During construction it was decided that, at this significant time in the development of the city, a building of presence was needed on such an important site. Shchusev was given the difficult task of redesigning the project through to completion.

Occupying an entire city block, the hotel faces both Theatralnaya and Manezhnaya squares. The main elevation faces Manezhnaya Ploshchad and the entrance to the recent underground shopping centre (see page 38). Here the building volume is broken down, giving focus to the lower pilastered block of the hotel entrance. On either side of the entrance the taller corners, expressed as two separate blocks, have been the focus of much folklore. Only the treatment of the fenestration is different on these otherwise uniform towers. Although the resulting asymmetry in an otherwise

A V Shchusev, L E Savelyev, O A Stapran 1935, 1976

A V Shchusev, L E Savelyev, O A Stapran 1935, 1976

balanced elevation was almost certainly a deliberate design decision on Shchusev's part, the alternative conjectures make far more interesting reading. Story one: Shchusev prepared two possible treatments for the façade, illustrating both on one drawing. When these were presented to Stalin for his decision, he approved and signed the drawing as shown. Because no one dared question his order, the hotel was built from the approved combination drawing. Story two: a pen squiggle by Stalin found on one side of the elevation drawing was thought to resemble three arched windows. Assuming this was an order, the hotel was built as per the altered drawing.

ADDRESS Manezhnaya Ploshchad
METRO Okhotny Ryad, Theatralnaya, Ploshchad Revolutsii

A V Shchusev, L E Savelyev, O A Stapran 1935, 1976

A V Shchusev, L E Savelyev, O A Stapran 1935, 1976

Apartment building (now Intourist offices)

One could be forgiven for thinking that the date given here must be wrong, but this classical building overlooking Manezhnaya Ploshchad really was designed and built a decade after Shukhov's radio tower (page 278), and is contemporary with buildings such as Melnikov's garage (page 202) and the Vesnin brothers' ZIL cultural palace (page 180).

Following the search for suitable housing types to accommodate the city's rapidly expanding population, the early 1930s saw the apartment block firmly established. For both political and practical reasons the constructivist philosophy of designing buildings from the inside out was replaced, and issues such as planning (which treated apartment buildings as blocks within the ensemble of the street) became dominant instead. In a complete reversal of constructivist ideals, the almost mandatory ostentation of the street façades now influenced interior layouts. This grandiose apartment building is probably the most extreme example of this approach, convincing many that the way forward lay in the past.

Zholtovsky, an academician and master of classicism, based the building on Andrea Palladio's 16th-century Villa Valmarana and Loggia del Capitaniato. He considered style a transient phenomenon, and saw the future in the rebirth of timeless classics in a pure state, without interpretation. This skilfully executed neo-classical structure with its gigantic architectural order was internally a cellular seven-storey residential building. It has now been refurbished internally and houses the offices of Intourist, the official tourist agency.

ADDRESS Mokhovaya Ulitsa, 15
METRO Okhotny Ryad

Around the Kremlin

I V Zholtovsky 1934

Around the Kremlin

I V Zholtovsky 1934

Manezhnaya Ploshchad

Development of the city in 1932 concentrated on the planning of urban spaces, including the widening of main thoroughfares as part of a new master plan for the Soviet capital. Focusing on Moscow's centre, this involved the creation of large urban spaces considered appropriate for the new large-scale structures of the time. One such space was Manezhnaya Ploshchad, situated beyond the Kremlin walls and bordering Alexandrovsky Sad (gardens). Until recently this was a vast asphalt wilderness, resulting from the demolition of small houses, estates and shops. In the 1930s there had been no nostalgia for the architectural heritage of the area – described at the time as 'ramshackle' with 'chaotic patterns' – as this was seen to stand in the way of progress.

Recent years have seen a second transformation of this urban space with the development, above a large underground shopping centre, of a linear plaza linking Manezhnaya Ploshchad and the Moskva Hotel.

The result of a competition, the winning project was a seven-storey-deep inverted tower, subsequently redesigned with a reduced number of levels. It is said this change was made not for obvious practical or commercial reasons, but because there was a possibility that it would interfere not only with the nearby metro lines but also with a private underground line to the Kremlin.

Revised by Mosproekt 2 with the assistance of foreign consultants, the new design focused on the commercial aspects of the development. The early treatment of the junction between the centre and Alexandrovsky Sad was drastically changed. Sloped arched openings which continued into the grassy banks of the adjoining gardens, respectfully maintaining the serenity of the place, were altered during construction and now finish vertically – their dressed marble columns separated from the gardens by an artificial river, and crowned with decorative stone balustrades. This

Mosproekt 2, Studio 11, B Ulkin, D L Lukaev (concept) 1993–97

Mosproekt 2, Studio 11, B Ulkin, D L Lukaev (concept) 1993–97

'embellishment' approach gains real momentum in the balconies and bridges around the river, supposedly a reminder of the nearby underground Neglinka river. A rich spatial quality has been achieved, and the use of water with attractive mosaic work by sculptor T S Tsereteli is lively and attractive. Unfortunately, the external treatment is so crassly decorated and over-ornamented with both architectural and sculptural elements that comparisons with Disneyland are appropriate.

Patterned stone paving decorates the surface of the plaza, which steps up in level towards the Moskva Hotel and is lit by a scattering of traditional lamp standards. Bronze ventilation shafts and stained-glass domes servicing the shopping mall below provide sizeable elements of ornament over this large area.

The 70,000-square-metre underground shopping complex is spread over four levels. Shopping is on three levels, with finishes in expensive marbles and metals. Heavily ornamented, the shopfronts dazzle the senses, their variety of garish styles a curious approach to retailing.

The park side of the complex has become a much-needed space in which to stroll and congregate in summer. However, it is a pity that, along with formality, taste and cultural heritage have also been ignored.

ADDRESS Manezhnaya Ploshchad
DESIGN WORK D L Lukaev; Mosinzhproekt: S Pakina
CHIEF ARTIST T S Tsereteli
CIVIL ENGINEERING Mosinzhstroy, Bauer (Germany)
METRO Ploshchad Revolutsii

Mosproekt 2, Studio 11, B Ulkin, D L Lukaev (concept) 1993–97

Mosproekt 2, Studio 11, B Ulkin, D L Lukaev (concept) 1993–97

Voskreseniya Vorota

Originally constructed in 1538, these gates formed the main entrance to the old part of the city (Kitay-Gorod) and were on the ceremonial route taken by the Tsars into Red Square. In 1680 the structure was rebuilt, with each pair of gates highlighted by a pitched roof, and their summits crowned with a double-headed eagle. An icon of the resurrection (voskreseniya) which hung over the gates gave them their present name. This peculiar structure was demolished in 1931 by order of Stalin to facilitate uninterrupted parades and Soviet army marching ceremonies from the widened Gorky Ulitsa (now Tverskaya Ulitsa) across the then newly formed Manezhnaya Ploshchad.

As part of the restoration of the Kitay-Gorod area, these gates and the adjoining small Iverskaya chapel were rebuilt, the design generally following that of the 1680 gates. However, changed proportions of openings and additional ornamentation highlighted with strong colour add nothing to the original. One positive aspect of this reinstatement is the re-enclosure of the north side of Red Square, but as with much reconstruction in the mid 1990s unselective pandering to the past by the Moscow authorities has left no room for a contemporary architectural interpretation. An opportunity to leave a signature of this time in the heart of the city has been lost.

Around the Kremlin

ADDRESS northern part of Red Square
METRO Theatralnaya

Mosproekt 2: O I Zhurin 1995

Mosproekt 2: O I Zhurin 1995

KGB administrative building

Sombre, unnumbered and unnamed, this eight-storey building stands between Lubyanka Ploshchad and Vorovskovo Ploshchad. The gun-metal-coloured granite cladding of the façade contrasts with the smooth black stone base crossing three discreet entrances. In dour colours reminiscent of military uniforms, this is not a building in which any jovial activity could be imagined; even a smile seems inappropriate as one passes under the constant watchful eye of the militia.

Crisp and sophisticated in its execution, this well-crafted building was part of an ensemble designed to complete and enclose the former Dzerzhinskovo Ploshchad. An administrative building for the KGB, it was designed as one of a pair of buildings (by the same architects) located on either side of the classical façade of the Lubyanka building (see page 52). Though similar in style, the earlier of the two (a computer building, also for the KGB) lacks the gravitas of its partner. The project, including the design of Dzerzhinskovo Ploshchad, was initiated in 1979 by Andropov, at that time head of the KGB. The square – a difficult design problem with seven points of access – was successfully concluded with a strong central focus, a large figurative monument of Felix Dzerzhinsky, the founder of the 'Cheka', later to become the KGB. Following the dissolution of the Soviet Union, the spontaneous release of long-suppressed emotions in the early 1990s saw the unceremonious removal of many figurative monuments to creators and leaders of Communist rule. Unfortunately (from an architectural perspective) this included the emotive figure of Dzerzhinsky.

The site of the new block was formerly occupied by three-storey buildings of little architectural merit (one housing the KGB medical department). These were demolished to make room for the new development, whose architectural treatment and scale derived from the scale of the

Mosproekt 2: B Paluy, G V Makarevich 1981

Mosproekt 2: B Paluy, G V Makarevich 1981

Lubyanka and the adjoining children's department store, Detsky Mir (Children's World).

The dark stone base to the façade, an interpretation of the rusticated base of the Lubyanka opposite, achieves a sculptural dynamic with deep recesses and geometric relief in its unwindowed walls. The lighter stone treatment of the floors above has a strong vertical emphasis contained by a labradorite stone cornice. Below the cornice, purpose-designed flagpole holders in labradorite appear as decorative dentils and, when hung with long vertical flags, add almost a sense of gaiety to the façade.

Less competent is an attempt made by the architects to reduce the scale where the new building meets the lower structures of Kuznetsky Most. A two-storey block projecting from the main rectangular structure was specifically designed to relate this monumental eight-storey building to its lower neighbours, but seems like a later addition.

ADDRESS Bolshaya Lubyanka Ulitsa
ASSOCIATED ARCHITECTS R Ambartsumian, Y Potashov, I Ivanov
METRO Lubyanka

Mosproekt 2: B Paluy, G V Makarevich 1981

Mosproekt 2: B Paluy, G V Makarevich 1981

Dinamo sports society building

Ivan Fomin, in the early 1920s the most influential of the Petrograd classicists, strove in his work to combine rationalist aesthetics and a strict design philosophy based on the classical orders. The intention of this approach was to learn from the cultural tradition of Russia and the discipline of classical architecture, using modern materials, changed proportions, and a simplicity more closely linked with the constructivists than traditional architecture. By the time he began working in Moscow in 1929 Fomin had developed this approach into a total design system, labelled 'proletarian classicism'.

Although designed as a club for the Dinamo sports society, the building includes residential accommodation, and is largely occupied at ground level by Moscow's biggest grocery store, known in Soviet times simply as 'grocery store number 40'. Intended originally for the *apparatchiks*, the store has over the years provided refreshments to architectural students from the nearby MARKhI (Moscow Architectural Institute). Dinamo's patrons were from the NKVD (later KGB), directly across the road. Muscovites have always referred to it as a KGB building, and this is reinforced to this day by a constant, if often discreet, police presence. Photography is prohibited, even of the residential block to the rear.

The stern and monumental colonnade along the main façades gives a strong symmetry to the corner administrative part of the building. Pairs of unembellished columns (without bases or capitals) are stylised as posts linking six storeys of the building, and are crowned by a flat deep cornice which forms the top floor. In a contrasting treatment, this level is largely solid, although pierced by a row of large circular windows, and overhangs the supporting columns below.

Fomin regarded paired columns – a basic component of proletarian classicism – as his personal artistic creation. The use of a single order

I A Fomin, A Y Langman 1928–29

I A Fomin, A Y Langman 1928–29

brought a unifying influence to multi-storey buildings, creating the effect of one monumental pile.

Sharply dividing the administrative and accommodation block which faces on to Furkasovsky Pereulok is a 14-storey tower. With its dynamic form, the apartment block differs from the adjoining administrative block in both presentation and expression.

The asymmetrical composition of the built complex has a constructivist spirit, but the original design intended the solution to be strictly symmetrical, with the volume of the main block repeated at the end of Furkasovsky Pereulok.

ADDRESS Bolshaya Lubyanka Ulitsa, 12
METRO Kuznetsky Most, Lubyanka

I A Fomin, A Y Langman 1928–29

I A Fomin, A Y Langman 1928–29

Lubyanka, KGB headquarters

On a corner site opposite the earlier Dinamo sports society building (in which Langman also participated), the Lubyanka possesses a very different architectural language. In the few years between the two constructions a dramatic change in architectural direction had begun to take place, with a move away from rationalist architecture towards the monumental classicism which was to dominate the next 30 years.

This building fills the remainder of a city block and adjoins Shchusev's classical reconstruction of a pre-revolutionary insurance building facing the former Dzerzhinskovo Ploshchad. Jointly, they form part of the notorious KGB headquarters identified in fact and fiction as the Lubyanka. During the period of Stalinist repression known as 'the purges', victims of night raids were brought to this building for interrogation and short-term incarceration before being despatched to the Gulags. What terrors these walls must have witnessed.

The walls in high-quality concrete and brick construction maintain a continuity of scale, and in their treatment establish a respectful relationship with their neighbour. However, by continuing the established parapet level and using a rusticated labradorite stone base at first-floor level, Langman articulates the building's individuality and presence in an expressive treatment which is quite modern in its architectural language. From the second to the eighth floor, triangular stone-faced fins give a vertical dynamic to the otherwise flat façade and echo the vertical emphasis of the Dinamo building opposite. The difficult junction with the earlier building is competently handled, with the elevation changing to dull plain render where they meet.

ADDRESS Bolshaya Lubyanka Ulitsa, 4
METRO Lubyanka

A Y Langman, I G Bezrukov 1934

A Y Langman, I G Bezrukov 1934

Around the Boulevard Ring

Christ the Saviour cathedral

In September 1997, as part of Moscow's 850th jubilee celebrations, the reconstructed Christ the Saviour cathedral was officially opened. On the same spot in 1883 the original cathedral had been consecrated, having taken more than 50 years to design and build. The recent construction, using modern mass concrete technology and based on the original design of K A Ton, was created under the direction of architect A Denisov in an incredible three years.

The original cathedral was situated on the site of a former monastery, on an embankment above the Moskva river, close to the Kremlin. Emulating the fate of many religious buildings during the Soviet period, the cathedral was blown up in 1931 to make way for the Palace of Soviets. Ornamental stones retrieved from the demolition were used in the decoration of buildings and metro stations under construction at that time.

Following several design competitions for the Palace of Soviets between 1931 and 1933, architects Boris Iofan, Vladimir Gelfreikh and Vladimir Shchuko were awarded the project. Their symbolic building, its telescopic form reminiscent of a tiered wedding cake, was composed of a series of stepped cylinders on a rectangular base, crowned by a giant statue of Lenin. Intended to be the largest building in the world, construction had reached little beyond foundation stage when stopped in 1942 by the Second World War.

The Palace project was eventually abandoned, and in 1960 it was decided to build an all-year outdoor swimming pool on the site. The existing foundations determined the shape and size of the pool – at 130 metres in diameter, the largest in the world – which was divided into several sections. Low buildings with changing rooms and other facilities around the perimeter followed the pool's curved outline. All were set in a park laid out as part of the development. Still in use in the early 1990s,

Mosproekt 2 (Studio 12): M M Posokhin, A M Denisov 1994–97

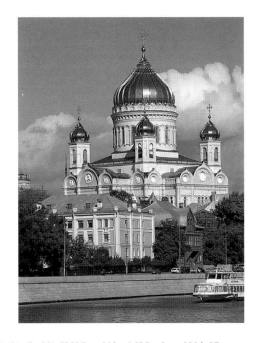

Mosproekt 2 (Studio 12): M M Posokhin, A M Denisov 1994–97

the heated pool was a curious sight in the heart of winter, with countless heads like white balls bobbing above a roof of mist which covered the huge area of water.

The enormous significance of the decision to reconstruct the cathedral – and its subsequent implementation – lay not so much in the reinstatement of a monument whose architectural value was debatable, but in its national, religious and political symbolism. Higher above the ground than its predecessor, the cathedral sits on a stylobate above the Hall of Church Assemblies. Below ground level, in addition to a church, there are refectories and car parking – satisfying late 20th-century requirements.

Stage-one construction of the building envelope was complete in 1997; in another three years it is planned that internal decoration and painting will be finalised. The interior work will include many fragments of the original, which have been saved and collected for this purpose. At night, with its sparkling gold-leaf-covered onion domes visible from many parts of the city, the cathedral is once again an integral part of the Moscow skyline – an icon for the Muscovites who funded the project entirely through private donations.

Around the Boulevard Ring

ADDRESS Volkhonka Ulitsa
ENGINEER V I Fadyeev
METRO Kropotkinskaya

Mosproekt 2 (Studio 12): M M Posokhin, A M Denisov 1994–97

Mosproekt 2 (Studio 12): M M Posokhin, A M Denisov 1994–97

Dom na Naberzhnoy

Towards the end of the 1920s, service and communal facilities started to make an appearance as an integral part of apartment infrastructure. This large complex, extending along Serafimovicha Ulitsa from Bersenevskaya Naberzhnaya to the Vodootvodny Canal, includes a supermarket, shop, canteen, gymnasium, library, theatre and cinema. The high-density complex has a building volume of 500,000 cubic metres on a 3-hectare site. One side of the complex faces on to the Moskva river.

Known as 'The House on the Embankment', the apartments were originally commissioned for the Kremlin élite – 'The Central Executive Committee' and the 'Soviet of National Commissars of the USSR'. Gloomy grey in colour, the exterior alluded to the fate of countless residents who only briefly enjoyed the privilege of life in this luxurious accommodation. Many, during the terror of Stalin's purges, were arrested in their homes by the NKVD (former KGB) and taken away, never to return. The individual apartments were identically furnished and fitted to the highest Soviet standard, with all the furnishings designed by the architects. The stern grey rendering, an effort to give the traditional brick façade the appearance of fashionable concrete construction, dulled an expressive and accomplished design. In 1997 this was remedied to some extent when the façade was repainted in lighter shades of grey.

Skilful massing of the complex cleverly resolves the dichotomy of its proximity to both the high red-brick walls of the Kremlin and the small-scale buildings of the adjoining historic district. The solution successfully relates the complex to both, in addition to creating a transition between these two zones. A complex configuration of 10- and 11-storey blocks housing 500 apartments is arranged asymmetrically around the perimeter of the site, which is divided internally by two blocks to form three courtyards, linked at ground level by two-storey-high archways. At the narrow

B M Iofan, D M Iofan 1928–31

B M Iofan, D M Iofan 1928–31

end of the site, the low form of the Udarnik cinema (now a showroom), with its expressive curved roof, relates in scale to the neighbouring district. On the embankment at the far side of the site, the impressive columned entrance of the Estrad theatre, contained by taller blocks, faces the Moskva river.

The repetitive module of the fenestration throughout the complex is broken by the vertical recesses of the balconies, creating an interesting rhythm – particularly successful in the composition of the courtyards.

ADDRESS Serafimovicha Ulitsa, 2–20
METRO Polyanka

B M Iofan, D M Iofan 1928–31

B M Iofan, D M Iofan 1928–31

Apartment building

Crisp and professional in its execution, this residential building is located on a corner site directly across from the Christ the Saviour cathedral. Its modern architectural expression is reminiscent of the nearby Moscow International Bank, also designed by the talented private studio of Alexander Skokan.

At seven storeys, its additional height above its four-storey neighbour is effectively diminished in the treatment of the façade. The flat rendered elevation of punched windows is interrupted from second to fifth level by balconies, their wire mesh crossing the vertical projected windows. On the top floor – in contrast, totally glazed – an overhanging fascia supported on fine steel columns effectively reduces the apparent height of the building.

The corner splayed towards the river is glazed in a disparate manner with an increased vertical emphasis. Less successful is the decisive rectangular massing of the building block, which appears particularly inconsiderate towards its immediate environment when viewed from the direction of the nearby Boulevard Ring.

Around the Boulevard Ring

ADDRESS Soymonovsky Proezd, 2–5
METRO Kropotkinskaya

Ostozhenka: D Gusev, A A Skokan, N Tokarev 1995–97

Ostozhenka: D Gusev, A A Skokan, N Tokarev 1995–97

Museum of Private Collections, Pushkin Museum of Fine Arts

As its name suggests, the museum was realised to house private collections, to be shown together and in their entirety. This new branch of the Pushkin Museum was created on the initiative of art historian Ilya Silberstein, who decided in 1985 to donate his private collection of more than 2000 pieces of Russian and west European art.

The building acquired to exhibit Silberstein's and other 'collections', occupies a corner site adjacent to the main museum, and was part of the former Golitsyn estate, which covered an architecturally important part of Moscow. It is now a preserved territory of 18th-century complexes, rich in cultural history. In 1887 S M Golitsyn rented out the ground floor and the left wing of this building as furnished apartments. From this time many famous writers and artists – including A Ostrovsky, I Bunin, V Surikov and I Repin – lived in number 14 and the adjoining buildings. From 1911 to 1933 Boris Pasternak lived with his family in the building on Volkhonka Ulitsa. After the revolution there was repeated replanning of the interiors, with the building being used as offices and apartments.

In 1987 when the building was given to the Pushkin, the design objective was to preserve, on the basis of archival research, the internal volumes and the façades while achieving the maximum exhibition space possible. This difficult brief has been resolved very successfully: the former living areas have become spacious yet intimate exhibition halls (achieved by preserving original walls), and the façades respond with restraint to their location.

As well as the main entrance to the museum at the narrow end of the building on Volkhonka Ulitsa, the old entrance on Znamensky Pereulok has been retained. The architects' idea was to create a main façade which was suitable for a public building yet respected the historical architecture

I M Vinogradsky, A N Ivanov, D V Bush, S N Chuklov 1988, 1993

Around the Boulevard Ring

I M Vinogradsky, A N Ivanov, D V Bush, S N Chuklov 1988, 1993

of the surrounding area. Treatment of the rendered façade with stone highlights gives a strong focus to the central doors, emphasised by full-height profiled stone cladding.

The main entrance at street level leads into a well-lit double-height space halfway between first- and basement-floor level, but unfortunately this entrance is not in daily use, and the dramatic sense of arrival achieved by the architects is thus not fully enjoyed.

Clever rearrangement of the internal spaces focuses around a bright and elegant central granite staircase contained by full-height walls, with natural light from above. Fragile glass-drop chandeliers designed by Igor Pyatkin hang over the stairwell – a reminder of his delicate watercolours, and the only decoration on this clearly defined main circulation route. Openings in the stair walls left and right at each level lead the visitor through a series of well-lit comfortably proportioned rooms displaying the collections. The route then returns to the stairwell to continue the ascent. The exhibition is organised so that the central staircase serves as the only ascent route, with one of the fire stairs being used for the return journey down to the cloakroom and café at basement level.

The main architect for the project was Vinogradsky. In 1991, after his death, the project was completed by colleagues. Designed and constructed at a time of great political upheaval and economic difficulty, it is commendable for its mood of quality and restraint.

ADDRESS Volkhonka Ulitsa, 14/1
ENGINEERS M Y Livshin, M M Berklaid
METRO Kropotkinskaya

I M Vinogradsky, A N Ivanov, D V Bush, S N Chuklov 1988, 1993

I M Vinogradsky, A N Ivanov, D V Bush, S N Chuklov 1988, 1993

ABC News

This restoration and development of a 19th-century former residence took place at a time of great change for the construction industry in Moscow, with a surge in building activity, and the appearance for the first time of developers. This activity included the conversion and upgrading of many existing buildings to 'western standards', in order to meet a new and growing market for office space in a burgeoning market economy.

At this difficult time the architects have skilfully realised the doubling of the area of the building, which now accommodates news and television studios. In doing so they have not only maintained the integrity of the original but have simultaneously given honest expression to the new structure.

The massing of the three-storey extension is concealed from the street by the vertical structure of the staircase, expressed as a separate element topped with a metal-columned cylindrical crown. The entrance set back from the original structure successfully joins new and old.

Around the Boulevard Ring

ADDRESS Bolshoy Afanasyevsky Pereulok, 7/1
RESTORER V Pavlov
METRO Kropotkinskaya

Architectural Studio ABD: A Bavykin, S Bavykin, B Levyant 1992–93

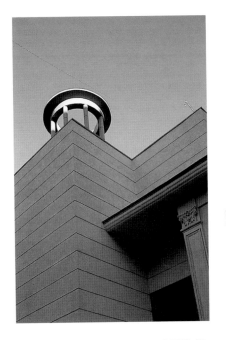

Around the Boulevard Ring

Architectural Studio ABD: A Bavykin, S Bavykin, B Levyant 1992–93

Dom Narkomata Oborny (GPU)

This defence-ministry building is unusually orientated in that its gable end faces on to the Boulevard Ring, whereas the main elevation – with a formidable protruding entrance portico – confronts a narrow side lane. The mass of the portico shadowing the entrance highlights the serious nature of the activities within the building, and its heavy bulk is relieved by two decorative panels in light-grey relief depicting stylised military tanks. Left and right of the portico, the buildings are crowned above a sandstone cornice with large obelisks, vertical decorative elements which are repeated around the perimeter of the roof. The building culminates in a high rectangular tower, reminiscent of an Italian campanile, decorated at high level with a combination of military symbols and grey corner stones.

Original in their style and character, the several volumes comprising this complex structure are delineated by the use of texture and colour. Above a smooth dull-grey stone plinth, the two lower floors have regular punched windows, and change texture in a defined diamond rustication. On the floor above – a contrast in rhythm and colour – pairs of circular sandstone columns separate larger windows, while the top five floors – in light grey with a cellular window pattern – sustain the horizontal emphasis. Characteristic of the art-deco style, there is an element of exaggeration in this beautifully executed building – from the balance of its masses to the details.

ADDRESS Gogolevsky Bulvar, 18
METRO Arbatskaya

L V Rudnev 1936

Around the Boulevard Ring

L V Rudnev 1936

Apartment building

The Stary Arbat is now a busy pedestrian shopping street. Its antiques and arts and crafts shops are particularly popular with tourists – as are the all-year-round souvenir stalls and the more recent addition of street cafés. Always associated with trade, the street now linking the Garden and Boulevard Rings originated in the 15th century as a trade road from Smolensk. In its 19th-century architectural heyday the district was known for its wooden Empire palaces, and up to the Second World War as a civilised intellectual environment. In 1986, the introduction of brick paving and lantern standards created the first pedestrian street in Moscow. Many consider the Europeanisation of an historic Russian street as the start of its downward spiral.

This new residential and commercial development is situated near the Boulevard Ring. It has apartments and artists' studios above ground-level retail units at ground level, it is stylistically in keeping with the Arbat of the 1990s. Above ground level the elevation is set well back from the street, allowing clear views of the quirky rendered façade and the oscillating roof line. The expressive treatment of the façade is achieved with a series of four adjoining irregular curved bays which run vertically to the various heights of the building and are articulated as separate elements with individual mansard roofs. The treatment of the metal roof is sheer fun – its lead colour contrasting with the sunny rendering of the façade, and its profile dynamic against the sky – providing an additional element of entertainment to the street activities below.

ADDRESS Stary Arbat Ulitsa, 19
METRO Arbatskaya

L Aranauskas 1996

L Aranauskas 1996

Novy Arbat Ulitsa

The Novy Arbat is a creation of the 1960s, though the plan for this main thoroughfare had been agreed as early as 1935. It was built with two main objectives: firstly to serve as one of the city's main radial arteries leading to the Kremlin, and secondly as a multi-functional centre intended as a focus of city life. It was previously called Kalinin Prospekt (along with many other streets, during the Soviet period it was named after a Soviet leader), but looked to the parallel street (Stary Arbat) for its new name.

Constructed in an old district between the Boulevard and Garden Rings, this development dwarfs the neighbouring streets and is visible across much of the city centre. Especially powerful visually is the south side of the Prospekt, which is formed by four 26-storey towers rising from a continuous stylobate over 800 metres in length. With four floors of accommodation, two above ground, the stylobate extends from the Arbat to the Garden Ring, encompassing shops, cafés, restaurants and, separately, entrances to the office towers. Distinctive in their form and juxtaposition, these towers, some occupied by government departments, have been described as a row of opened books. Their solid gables facing towards the Kremlin transform the street when decorated with the long colourful banners hung out for holidays and parades.

On the northern side of the prospekt the design of five separate residential towers – named after the retail premises occupying their lower floors – is more static. The strip geometry of these buildings is relieved by the signage of their five names. In individual letters – eye-catching and to the point in the pre-neon, pre-advertising Soviet era – they spell out Dom Knigi (The House of Books), Cinema October, Melodia, Siren (a perfume shop), and The Malachite Box (a jewellery shop). Three decades after its construction, this monotonous overbearing design is recognised as an architectural and social disaster, alien to the structure of the city.

M V Posokhin et al 1962–68

M V Posokhin et al 1962–68

Amid great excitement the first private supermarket and public house (The Irish House) in Moscow were opened in the stylobate in 1991. Since then there have been many internal changes, including a small shopping centre and department store (The British House). At the same time as the prospekt was responding to retail demand with the provision of new products, it became littered with kiosks, a blight repeated in many parts of the city. Many of these have since been removed as more retail space became available. In addition, this type of development has been curtailed by the questionable decision of the Moscow authorities to construct controlled kiosk developments.

In recent years various proposals have been prepared to improve the prospekt and its use, particularly at street level and below, with the aim of humanising the environment while providing needed facilities and additional shopping. This design work, with no present time-scale for its realisation, is being prepared by the state architectural bureau Mosproekt 2, under the direction of Mikhail Mikhailovich Posokhin, son of the original architect.

ADDRESS Novy Arbat Ulitsa, 247–300
ASSOCIATED ARCHITECTS A A Mndoyants, G V Makarevich, B I Tkhor, S A Airapetov, Y V Popov, I A Pokrovsky, A V Zaitsev
ENGINEERS A V Ratskevich, S Y Shkolnikov
METRO Arbatskaya

M V Posokhin et al 1962–68

M V Posokhin et al 1962–68

Mosselprom building

Construction started in 1911 to the design of N D Strukov. In 1913 it was partially destroyed and was finally completed by D M Kogan after the October revolution: This possibly explains why the treatment of the façade is reminiscent of apartment buildings at the start of the century.

Situated at a corner of three lanes, the narrow end of the building at their junction is terminated by a dentilated tower. At 11 storeys, the block was one of the highest public buildings constructed in Moscow during the 1920s, though its position – set back down a narrow lane at a Y junction from the main street – reduced the apparent height. In 1997 the left-hand side of the street approaching the building was completely demolished, totally distorting the intended perception of the block.

An interesting aspect of this building, unfortunately no longer in evidence, was its applied decoration in the form of advertising for Mosselprom, the government agency set up to distribute and promote the city's food supply. In the early days of Communism, when competition from private suppliers still existed, a bright advertising sign decorated the building, with text written by the revolutionary poet Mayakovsky. Across one wall were the words 'nowhere else but in Mosselprom', while the left part of the building featured 'yeast, cigarettes, beer and waters, biscuits, sweets, chocolate'. In addition to these words there were drawings illustrating the products. Apart from this decoration the front walls were painted in two colours, with horizontal elements underlined in a dark colour and verticals in a light colour to exaggerate the relief of the building. The top of the tower was crowned by text and a clock.

ADDRESS Nizhny Kislovsky Pereulok, 297
METRO Arbatskaya

B D Tsvetayev 1923–25

Around the Boulevard Ring

B D Tsvetayev 1923–25

Dom Polyarnikov (House of the Polar Explorers)

This residential building facing on to the Boulevard Ring has a cream rendered façade decorated in stylised motifs derived from classical architecture. The central block, set back and higher than the overlapping two sides, has an elevational treatment which is separated into three horizontal layers. At the lower and middle level it is divided by pilasters forming a portico, and at the upper levels by three deep balconies. Focus towards the central entrance block is further emphasised by the vertical rows of recessed balconies and tiers of pilasters. A very important element in the appearance of the building are the cornices which rest on carved wooden rafters. These give the building a southern character and, together with elegant galleries and narrow columns, reflect the influence of the late Italian renaissance. The villa style with its elegant shallow-pitched overhanging roof is also reminiscent of Moscow art nouveau.

The symmetry of the elevation is interrupted at ground-floor level on the left-hand corner, where a doorway from an earlier turn-of-the-century building has been retained and the older building amalgamated into the new, maintaining its original higher ceilings. The key-hole-shape entrance gives the front elevation a light and pleasant asymmetry.

The almost mandatory decorative and grandiose approach to façades at this time is also reflected in the internal layout. In 1932 the statutory size and height of individual living space was increased; in theory this should have resulted in improved standards of living, with spacious comfortable high-ceilinged apartments, such as in this building. However, these large apartments proved an uneconomical solution to the continuing and ever-increasing housing shortages. As a result, in many buildings such as this, married couples were each allocated a room, with shared kitchen and bathroom facilities. As children were born, these rooms

E L Iokheles 1936–37

E L Iokheles 1936–37

became communal apartments with whole families living in each one. In recent times many of these apartments have reverted to single occupancy. The plan of this building included a variety of apartment layouts; a creche was also intended at first-floor level, though was not realised. Iokheles himself lived in this block, in a more modest apartment at attic level.

Originally the building was commissioned for the families of senior members of the Moscow Navy, and was known as the Apartment Building of the Main Northern Sea Route. However, on the successful return of the Soviet explorers from their Arctic expedition, Stalin, in appreciation of their achievements, allocated this building to these pioneers and their families, renaming it the House of the Polar Explorers. In popular Soviet style, large portraits of these Soviet heroes hung from the balconies, and to this day the central entrance has a small exhibition devoted to the former famous residents.

Around the Boulevard Ring

ADDRESS Nikitisky Bulvar, 9
METRO Arbatskaya

E L Iokheles 1936–37

E L Iokheles 1936–37

MKhAT (Moscow Arts Theatre)

Construction of a musical theatre began on this site in the 1930s, but the process was interrupted by the Second World War. In 1960, with the recommencement of the project, it was decided to create a new building for the popular Moscow Arts Theatre (MKhAT), then in a building in Kamergesky Pereulok by the art-nouveau architect Fedor Shekhtel.

Facing on to the Boulevard Ring in a neighbourhood of elegantly detailed small-scale period buildings, the site was not suitable either to accommodate or service a building of this type. A further complication was the need to retain part of the earlier theatre construction. Nevertheless, in an innovative response, away from the largely anonymous buildings of this period, the designers created a powerful monumental mass.

The slightly glum, predominantly horizontal accent of the building makes it totally different from its neighbours, as does the dour brown colour of its tuff stone facing. In contrast, an over-energetic dynamism is given to the façade by beautifully detailed lantern lights which spring out and up from the columns as though on extensible arms. The upper levels of the façade, in horizontally stepped bands of rough-cut solid stone, were designed to symbolise a lowered theatre curtain. Narrow copper-clad columns support the upper levels, while a concrete balcony, supported between the columns horizontally, divides the bottom two levels and shelters the entrance below.

While working on the project, its authors tried to incorporate traditional associations with the original theatre building in the ornamentation and colour schemes of the interior design; in all else the monumental building appears absolutely alien in its classical surroundings.

ADDRESS Tverskoy Bulvar, 20–22
METRO Pushkinskaya

V S Kubasov, V S Ulyashov 1960–74

Around the Boulevard Ring

V S Kubasov, V S Ulyashov 1960–74

Izvestia offices

Grigory Barkhin's first proposals for the offices and printing works for *Izvestia* (news) featured a central tower. This early design was rejected as it was thought it would overpower its neighbours. The revised building occupies an infill site along the Boulevard Ring overlooking Pushkin Square, and integrates pleasingly with its environment. An editorial block immediately to the left, built in 1975, takes its height from the original, while the two-storey period building to the right offers a glimpse of the original impact of this industrial and administrative facility.

A complex structural solution was necessary to combine the disparate spatial requirements of the publishing and printing departments in one building. Resolved using a concrete frame, this structural module also provides the basis for the organisation of the façade. In spite of this restrictive grid and an almost square façade, the asymmetry of the revised design maintains the dynamism of the earlier scheme. This is achieved by an unbroken vertical band of glazing over the main entrance and a series of projecting solid balconies crossing the modular fenestration.

The treatment changes on the top (sixth) floor, with four large porthole windows in the solid wall to the offices of the editor and chief. Further depth is given to the elevation by the organisation of the left-hand corner where a clock and the treatment at roof level give the impression of a tower to those approaching the premises from the left.

Rationalist in its approach, and entirely functional in its realisation, characteristic elements of constructivism have been orchestrated to achieve an expressive, attractive composition. Grigory designed this project with his son Mikhail early in their 25-year working relationship.

ADDRESS Pushkinskaya Ploshchad, 5
METRO Pushkinskaya, Tverskaya, Chekhovskaya

G B (and M G) Barkhin 1925–27

Around the Boulevard Ring

Around the Boulevard Ring

G B (and M G) Barkhin 1925–27

TRAM restaurant

Below the Lenkom Moscovsky theatre building, discreetly announced at street level by a criss-cross railing, is the entrance to this cosmopolitan basement restaurant. Restaurant-cafés are a popular and relatively recent arrival to Moscow, their decor mainly of the themed or nostalgic variety. Standing out from these packaged designs is the creative solution hinted at in the name of this restaurant, 'TRAM' – Theatre Restaurant for Moscow Actors. This dramatic interior, a little pretentious perhaps, has an atmosphere more reminiscent of Paris than Moscow. Arriving in the neutral tones of the café-bar, one meets a gently vaulted dark lacquered ceiling and an imaginative play of wall planes. Patterns and furniture here appear to aspire to Philippe Starck.

In the adjoining small restaurant two side walls are padded in dark velvet and buttoned with tiny lights. Replicating a cinema booth, the ceiling above and the floor below step down in a series of eating levels towards a cinema screen showing black and white movies to entertain those bored with their dinner companions. The changes in level coupled with the dim lighting are not altogether practical; however, it is imaginative and pleasantly different. Unfortunately the crisp unadorned design does not continue beyond the main spaces; the recreational rooms behind the restaurant have obviously been implemented without the architect's skilful input.

ADDRESS Malaya Dmitrovka Ulitsa, 6
METRO Pushkinskaya, Chekovskaya

Y Andreev 1996

Y Andreev 1996

MKhAT apartment building

Monumental in both its massing and its decorative imagery, this building represents the ideologised image of the new Communist Moscow of the 1930s. It is built in a mixture of art-deco style and adapted classical elements. The almost flat façade of this large building facing on to a lane is given mass, importance and depth by an expressive stepped-up tower, deep-set balconies, and a cornice supported by round columns with simplified Doric capitals. The balconies connect four windows – two vertically and two horizontally.

An elegant vehicular arch below the tower features an unusual relief, its theme representing the happy life of the Soviet people (sculpture by G Motovilov). In contrast to the grey granite facing of the lower floors, the reliefs are in a light yellow stone.

Coloured deco motifs at other entrances to the building also breathe life into the elevation. Plaques to many of the famous artists who lived in the building, many of whom worked in the nearby Bolshoy Theatre, add further decoration to the façade.

ADDRESS Glinishchevsky Pereulok, 5–7
METRO Chekovskaya

V N Vladimirov 1935–37

V N Vladimirov 1935–37

MVD clinic and apartment building

The composition of this corner clinic and residential building was influenced by Le Corbusier and resulted in an external treatment that is one of the best examples of late constructivism. A fusion of two equal-height intersecting volumes, the building consists of a short deep block (housing a government clinic) set back from Petrovka Ulitsa, and a long narrow residential block along Petrovsky Pereulok, continuing beyond the shorter building to the street corner. Expressing the structure in an almost industrial repetitive rhythm, the monotony of the fenestration along its length is broken by the solid thin projections of cantilevered balconies, their fine metal rails almost invisible against the rendered façade. Combined with the treatment of the curvilinear corners of the residential block, the building achieves a rhythmic diversity. The rounded elevation at the street corner is wrapped with continual horizontal bands of windows which establish a strong horizontal emphasis, while on the same elevation the recessed balconies of the curved inner corner add depth and variety to the otherwise flat façade.

Rationalism is abandoned at the entrance porch, where energetic geometric patterns on red and white stone walls lead into a white marble reception, whose classical treatment is indicative of the path architecture was taking at this time under Stalin's direction.

ADDRESS Petrovka Ulitsa, 25a
METRO Chekovskaya

N I Pozhdestvensky, E Grebenshchikov 1934

N I Pozhdestvensky, E Grebenshchikov 1934

Sovmortrans office complex

Gay and colourful amid its duller neighbours, this administrative/hotel building for Sovmortrans (Marine House) is situated on Rachmanovsky Pereulok, in an old part of the city which is considered more European than Russian in its architectural style. The immediate environment of the complex, which occupies a previously empty site, comprises mainly turn-of-the-century buildings given over to large trade, administrative and public organisations.

The new building repeats the curve of the street in its long façade, and blends smoothly into the volumes of the adjoining façades. Inventively, the central entrance is expressed in curved glazing which extends the full height of the building, set back and traversed by metal glass-floored balconies. Where the long elevation changes direction, taking up the street line left and right of this pivotal point, the imagery is reminiscent of a giant hinge. Either side of the entrance above second-floor level is a solid, white rendered façade with cellular windows, slightly proud of the remainder of the elevation. It gives the impression of two large panels supported by square red granite-clad columns below.

Set back to form a deep recess, the first floor incorporates access to the car park. This is unobtrusive in the shadow of the overhang, which also, usefully, partially screens the less accomplished curtain wall treatment at this level. The overhang in addition acts as a shelter to the main doors, entered at an angle to the street. This unusual location allows the regular structural grid of the building to continue without interruption. A column is positioned at the centre point where one would normally expect to find the entrance doors.

In image, colour and volume one can clearly see marine references in this 11,000-square-metre building, considered by Moscow architects at the time of its construction as 'super modern' in style. Its architectural

V Kolosnitsin, M Okunev, I Kochetova 1995

V Kolosnitsin, M Okunev, I Kochetova 1995

language, then new to Moscow, was a little over-enthusiastic in places, using a palette of colours and some elements borrowed from Michael Graves in its multi-coloured rendered façade.

The design and configuration of the elevation would appear to have taken into consideration the fact that the long façade is primarily viewed at an oblique angle from Petrovka Ulitsa. Overall, the use and play of elements has had the effect of widening this narrow street.

ADDRESS Rakhmanovsky Pereulok, 4
ENGINEERS S Kozyrenko (Russia), P Leibetseder, P Habrik (Austria)
METRO Kuznetsky Most

V Kolosnitsin, M Okunev, I Kochetova 1995

Around the Boulevard Ring

V Kolosnitsin, M Okunev, I Kochetova 1995

Stary Tsirk (Old Circus)

It is known as the Old Circus to distinguish it from the circular Novy Tsirk (New Circus), constructed in 1971 on Vernadskovo Prospekt by V Khavin. This more recent development, adjacent to the central market, evolved from the Moscow Circus which was established about 100 years ago. The original 1880 structure designed by A E Veber, although of no significant architectural merit, was held in great esteem by performers and audiences alike – and Krasilnikov took this into consideration in his design solution. Yuri Nikulin, director of the circus until his death in 1997, was one of Russia's most well-known personalities, famous both as a film actor and as a former clown in the circus.

The circus opens daily at noon, from which time the entrance steps and nearby footpaths are crowded with traders and hordes of young Muscovites with their minders.

The main architectural feature of the enlarged circus (which seats 1800) is the incorporation of preserved fragments from the original building. They are visible in areas such as the centre of the boulevard façade and in some elements of the main performance hall. The new façade encloses the original, framing it in a bevelled halo of tinted glass on three sides and steps from the street level.

Extending to the rear of the site is the new development providing improved facilities. Unfortunately, its side façade on to the market, articulated in a modern architectural language, may soon be screened by another development. For the moment, the new structure blends in comfortably with the historic boulevard.

ADDRESS Tsvetnoy Bulvar, 13
ENGINEER I Mirimanov
METRO Tsvetnoy Bulvar

Around the Boulevard Ring

V D Krasilnikov, A A Agafonov, N Kudryashev 1988

V D Krasilnikov, A A Agafonov, N Kudryashev 1988

Lucoil office building

Built in 1900 as a jewellery factory, in Soviet times this building was used for apartments, before eventually falling into disuse. In 1991 reconstruction began, and two years later the derelict industrial building had been transformed into the head offices of an oil company, with its floor area increased by 40 per cent.

This elegant building is positioned at right angles to Zvonarsky Pereulok, partly hidden from the street behind an unrenovated block. However, the treatment of the new façade, added to the gable of the original structure, and the handling of the large forecourt give the building a suitable presence. Faced in red brick, the new elevation matches the restored original walls; the distinctive use of brick in this type of building is combined with glazed ceramic panels. The Pavlovs developed this synthesis of art and architecture from traditional Russian church and residential design of the 17th to the 19th century. These decorative elements on the main gable façade combine with a tall arched window to give a strong focus to the main entrance below.

If one were to categorise this building within a genre it would be 'New Russian'. The architectural approach here is modern yet definitively Russian in style, drawing on a combination of historic cultural traditions, and the architectural experience of the architects. Peter Pavlova, who worked on this project with his daughter Marina, is a master of ritualistic buildings including mortuaries and crematoria. This experience can be recognised in his handling of the building envelope and is especially noticeable in the profile of the roof.

ADDRESS Zvonarsky Pereulok, 5
ARTIST O A Ikonnikov
METRO Kuznetsky Most

P P Pavlov, M P Pavlova 1991–93

P P Pavlov, M P Pavlova 1991–93

Government Investment Corporation

Built as the offices of the Ministry for Radio Technology, the long and narrow mass of this new building joins perpendicularly to a 19th century structure facing on to Sakharov Prospekt. The main façade of the new structure decisively and determinedly terminates and links both Sakharov Prospekt and the parallel Myasnitskaya Ulitsa. This nine-storey concrete-frame and brick structure takes its scale from the buildings on Sakharov Prospekt behind, including Le Corbusier's Tsentrosoyuz (see page 106). A massive façade faces on to the Boulevard Ring: framed with a heavy stone band surround, it has the appearance of a stage proscenium. Set inside this frame, the flat elevation – composed of crossing vertical and horizontal elements in deep relief – combines with solid semi-circular balconies to create an interestingly articulated façade. This dextrous treatment is characteristic of the 1970s. Facing on to and set back from Turgenevskaya Ploshchad on the Boulevard Ring, the building has a monumentality which dominates the square.

ADDRESS Myasnitskaya Ulitsa, 35
METRO Turgenevskaya, Chistye Prudy

D S Solopov, L Abrameytsev, V Ivanov 1973–82

D S Solopov, L Abrameytsev, V Ivanov 1973–82

Tsentrosoyuz building

In 1926 Mossovet allocated a 12,000-square-metre site to Tsentrosoyuz, the Central Union of Consumers' Co-operatives. A decade later, following several architectural competitions, technical development difficulties and a period of suspension of the construction works, Le Corbusier's only realised design in the Soviet Union was completed. Under a cloud of ridicule even before its completion, it was not until the Khrushchev era that Le Corbusier's architectural reputation, like that of many Soviet dissidents, was eventually reinstated.

In an old district of Moscow dominated by classical architecture, the Tsentrosoyuz and a number of contemporary buildings are the stylistic exceptions. Moreover, it was during the period of construction of this modernist building that political trends changed drastically, and architecture began to withdraw its brief patronage of the avant-garde in favour of traditional neo-classicism.

The largest office block in the city at the time of construction, the complex housed the headquarters of the Central Union. During construction it was renamed the Narkomlegprom building, and the design altered to accommodate 2500 workers. Three rectangular blocks of offices positioned almost perpendicular to each other wrap around a fourth, curved recreational structure housing a large entrance hall and auditorium.

Designed with a dual orientation (following a conscious decision not to create a primary façade), the rigid office buildings face on to the existing Myasnitskaya Ulitsa. The softer form of the recreational complex – given a different architectural treatment but of equal importance – was orientated towards the proposed Sakharov Prospekt, eventually built almost 50 years later. Raised on pilotis, the stone and glass walled seven-storey commercial service block is set back from the narrow and once-busy Myasnitskaya Ulitsa, flanked at either end by blocks one storey

Le Corbusier, N D Kolli 1929–36

Le Corbusier, N D Kolli 1929–36

higher. The colour of the tuff stone which clads the reinforced-concrete structure is recorded as red: today it could be more accurately described as an impolite shade of brown, dulling the overall impression of the structure.

Le Corbusier and his cousin Pierre Jeanneret intentionally avoided the traditional organisation of office blocks around courtyards; instead they used a series of angular planes to align the blocks and achieve maximum penetration of natural light. Other innovative features proposed included new solutions to the problems of heating and ventilation, but in the event these proved impractical and were never realised. Also, ramps and paternoster lifts had been intended as the exclusive means of horizontal and vertical circulation; although some ramps were realised, these were in addition to the staircases in the building rather than replacements.

The Soviet architect Nikolai Kolli was involved from an early stage in the development of the project, and later mediated between Le Corbusier's high-tech aspirations and the relatively primitive resources available within the Soviet construction industry. After his third trip to Moscow in 1930, and despite continued effort, Le Corbusier was unable to secure further invitations to visit the site. Kolli, who assumed complete responsibility for the luminous interiors, used a variety of marble and oak detailing to offset the severity of the exterior.

Despite large-scale modifications to some elements of the interior, the finished building has remained relatively faithful to the original design.

Around the Boulevard Ring

ADDRESS Myasnitskaya Ulitsa/Akademika Sakharova Prospekt
METRO Turgenevskya, Chistye Prudy, Krasnye Vorota

Le Corbusier, N D Kolli 1929-36

Le Corbusier, N D Kolli 1929–36

Around the Garden Ring

Mezhdunarodny Moscow bank

In the 1920s, Palaces to the Workers constituted the main building form, offering the potential for individual architectural expression while simultaneously articulating the ideologies of society. In the 1990s it is banks which hold this position. The Moscow International Bank, the first and best example of this building type, appeared in the embryonic days of democracy. It is also one of the finest examples of contemporary architecture in the city. One of the difficulties facing the architects at the onset of this commission was the novelty of such a building type.

Situated on the banks of the Moskva river directly across from the Central House of the Artists, the bank relates comfortably to its 19th-century neighbours in a clearly articulated modern architectural language. Four floors of the front façade constitute a single solid element aligning with the adjacent buildings. Above this level the dissociated increased scale of the new structure is set back, its totally glazed façade covered in a shallow curved metal-sheeted roof.

The building occupies a site on the corner of Prechistenskaya Naberezhnaya (formerly Kropotkinskaya) and Korobeynikov Pereulok, and is more than 16,000 square metres in area, including two levels of underground parking. This was the first large-scale building executed in accordance with the planned regeneration of the Ostozhenka Ulitsa area, positively realising the concept of enlarging business and social activities in the region. The authors' tactful insertion in this old part of the city imposes a new architectural identity on the embankment.

The shape of the plan is an irregular rectangle dictated by the historical borders of the site, which had in turn been ordained by the line of a now-underground stream. The volume of the six-storey structure is divided into two parts. The massive lower treatment, a combination of stone and dark brick, contrasts with the metal-framed glazing of the remaining top

Ostozhenka: A A Skokan, V V Kanyashin, R S Baishev 1991–95

Around the Garden Ring

Ostozhenka: A A Skokan, V V Kanyashin, R S Baishev 1991–95

third. However, the façade facing on to the central yard is divided into three parts, which affords a better relationship with the lower scale of the surrounding buildings.

The compositional centre and dominant feature of the interior is the atrium, which allows light to penetrate the depth of the building. In both interior and exterior, modern building technology is skilfully explored, with materials such as glass in large sheets, stone and steel components fusing in an ascetic design.

ADDRESS Prechistenskaya Naberezhnaya
ASSOCIATED ARCHITECTS Y Pallasmaa, Davidson & Linberg Architects (Finland)
METRO Park Kultury

Ostozhenka: A A Skokan, V V Kanyashin, R S Baishev 1991–95

Ostozhenka: A A Skokan, V V Kanyashin, R S Baishev 1991–95

Finnish Embassy extension

In 1935, following a design competition, the commission for the embassy was awarded to second-prize-winner, Hilding Ekelund. However, with Stalinist classicism the firmly established style at that time, the Moscow authorities found his functionalist façade unacceptable. The revised design, completed in 1939, remained faithful to the original concept.

Commissioned in 1989, the crisp and contemporary annex respects both Ekelund's earlier work and the neighbouring Australian Embassy, an art-nouveau building designed by Shekhtel in 1904. The new block consists of a short wing on to the street, parallel to the existing building, and, perpendicular to it on the east of the site, a longer wing enclosing most of the garden park and forming a protected courtyard.

Immediately adjoining Ekelund's building, the new reinforced-concrete structure has render over plastered masonry walls, painted to match. The basic orthogonal geometry of the original windows is repeated, but in a relaxed manner allowing the occasional irregularity. The external corner adjoining its Australian neighbour is more high-tech and set back from the main façade. In time, a lightweight steel trellis designed as a framework for climbing vines should form a soft green junction between old and new.

In addition to the consular section to the front of the site, new facilities include a multi-purpose hall, dining room, library, swimming pool, sauna, and four apartments. Rich spatial diversity in the interior is highlighted by the confident use of colour and a variety of materials. The overall impact is chic, modern and definitively Finnish.

ADDRESS Kropotkinsky Pereulok, 11
ENGINEERS A Insinoorit Ltd, V Kilpeläinen
METRO Kropotkinskaya

Around the Garden Ring

Helin & Slitonen 1995

Helin & Slitonen 1995

Novosti press centre

Constructed as the press centre for the 22nd Olympic games, the composition of the complex was influenced by the neighbouring Proviantskiye food stores, elegant 1830s buildings by F Shestakov (to the design of V Stasov). Their proximity, however, created a difficult task for the architects. Though not immediately apparent, the lower floors of the press centre's façade line through with the overall height of the food stores. Elongated stone-clad columns carry the upper floors of the seven-storey structure, giving it a monumental image. Special attention was given to the treatment of the corners, where massive posts appear to pierce through the top of the building.

Four large columned openings lead from the street into three interior courtyards. Here, in contrast to the rigid lines of the building envelope, the massing is softened by the expressed volume of the recreational facilities, including a conference hall

With its horizontal dynamic, and upper floors jutting out over lower levels suspended over an elongated structure, the shape of the building is characteristic of a 1970s approach. Different interpretations of this architectural manner can be seen in MKHAT (see page 86), the Moskvich Palace of Culture, and Moscow Univermag.

ADDRESS Zubovsky Bulvar, 4
ARCHITECTS I M Vinogradsky, V K Antonov, A S Dubovsky, V M Orlov, Y V Kalmykov, Y Yuzim
ENGINEERS M M Berklaid, E Soldatov, S Khadzhibaromov, A Belyaev, N Gorshkova
METRO Park Kultury

Various architects 1977–80

Around the Garden Ring

Various architects 1977–80

Mikhail Frunze military academy

Symbolic imagery is typical of the work of Lev Rudnev; this military academy, designed together with Viktor Munts, is one of his most spectacular buildings. Based on spatial contrasts, clarity and tranquil force are the hallmarks of this composition. Everything in its imagery, articulated in the solidity, strength and monumentality of the building, expresses the greatness and invincibility of the Soviet army.

This impressive complex consists of three compositional elements: a main monolithic coffered volume over a closed stylobate, plus a heavy cubed pedestal cut into the stylobate. These collectively form a single sculptural entity. The massing and rhythmical contrasts, using carefully worked out proportions, give definition and balance to the overall composition, with each of the elements interconnecting harmoniously.

The laconic ten-storey block of the main building, embellished by a cellular pattern of caisson windows, contrasts with the solid horizontal white stone stylobate at first-floor level. This is separated from the pavement by a continuous narrow band of glazing, broken at regular intervals by polished black granite posts. Hammer and sickle reliefs in a widely spaced rhythm of cubes decorate the massive wall of the stylobate, while on the stone pedestal one can just about see quotations (from Stalin) etched into the face of the stone. Originally the pedestal was crowned with a wooden model of a pre-war tank, its front rising up in a threatening gesture. This eventually rotted and fell apart, and was not replaced.

Around the Garden Ring

ADDRESS Devichevo Polya Proezd, 4
METRO Frunzenskaya, Park Kultury

L V Rudnev, V O Munts 1931–37

L V Rudnev, V O Munts 1931–37

Kauchuk factory club

Melnikov designed this building as a club house for the Moscow rubber factory. On a corner site, the mass of the main rendered-brick block is diagonally set back from the street junction, employing a volume of two radiating part-cylinders to express the semi-circular 800-seat auditorium. Corridors encircling this space act as foyers to club rooms on the outer cylinder. Vertical strips of glazing on the elevation contrast with the higher, almost solid, inner cylinder of the auditorium. A separate cylindrical structure houses the box office and vestibule. Smaller and lower, it juts out beyond the main volume to address the corner of the two streets bordering the site. An external double circular staircase wraps around this compact independent building, and joins the smaller structure to the main block.

In a totally different interpretation, the expression of the mass of the auditorium and the use of external stairs (doubling as a reviewing stand during Soviet rallies) can be observed in another Melnikov design of the same period, the Rusakov House of Culture (see page 214).

The building still operates as a club, but its interior has reverted to classicism, particularly evident in the treatment of the main auditorium. Here a romantic painted ceiling, a crystal chandelier, cornices, pilasters and the decorative treatment of the two tiered balconies are all a later, unwelcome, addition to the original rationalist aesthetic.

ADDRESS Ulitsa Plyushchikha, 64
METRO Frunzenskaya, Park Kultury

Around the Garden Ring

K S Melnikov 1927–29, 1970

K S Melnikov 1927–29, 1970

Apartment building

The block is directly across the river from Kievsky railway station, in pre-neon blitz Moscow. I innocently thought it was 'the Camel building', due to what I now realise is a yellow neon advertisement sitting like a crown above its roof line. Designed in the 1930s for the Nomenklatura (middle-ranking Soviet officials), the building is known as 'the architects' house' because of the number of architects residing there.

An example of social realism in neo-Greek-Russian-classical style, this building's interest also stems from the potential of its unfulfilled design. Shchusev died in 1949, at which time only three fifths of the crescent had been built. To the left and right of the central crescent-shaped block, two wings with open colonnades were planned to run parallel to the river, their vertical rhythm continuing beyond the gables of the main block. The flat blocks which now crudely abut on the central structure are totally lacking in such elegance. Shchusev's central block originally embraced a small 19th-century church, but this was demolished in the late 1950s.

The refined proportions of the façade change tempo towards the top of the building. Although at the upper levels this tiered approach lacks the modelling and articulation of the roof line exhibited in the sketch design, it does maintain the spirit of Shchusev's original concept.

It was also intended that the complex should have a strong relationship with the Moskva river below, to be achieved by a series of steps and terraces on the embankment in front of the building. The landscaping was never realised, and with time the concept seems to have been conveniently forgotten. Furthermore, lamentable plans are afoot to develop this long narrow strip of green space dividing the building from the waterfront.

ADDRESS 7th Rostovsky Pereulok, 5
METRO Smolenskaya

A V Shchusev (first part) 1936–62

Around the Garden Ring

A V Shchusev (first part) 1936–62

MID (Ministry of Foreign Affairs)

Distinctive among the Moscow skyscrapers for its restrained decoration and definitive composition, the 27-storey, 172-metre-high offices for the Ministry of Foreign affairs and the Ministry for Trade of the Russian Federation elegantly preside over Smolenskaya-Sennaya Ploshchad, enjoying an open panorama over the Moskva river. Terminating the perspective from the Borodinsky Bridge, it forms part of a square symmetrically flanked by an overpowering pair of bland 1970s towers (surprisingly, created by the same architects as the MID building). These two towers, the Belgrade and the Zolotoe koltso (golden ring) hotels, are known as Belgrade 1 and 2.

The Stalin towers, of which the MID is one – grand architectural gestures intended to be the only high-rise buildings in the city centre – were apparently inspired by Manhattan skyscrapers. In the case of the MID, a neo-gothic New York hospital would seem to be more than a distant relation.

The building has a light external stone wall concealing a strong carcass construction. Its walls, decorated in projecting vertical pylons, portray one of the motifs of the unrealised Palace of Soviets, a project on which Gelfreikh had worked with Iofan. The significantly projecting pilasters define the tower's monumental volume in a vertical imagery executed with consistency and boldness over its entire height. The effect is almost austere in comparison with the other skyscrapers. Though larger than most of the surrounding buildings, its gradual increase in height (from six storeys at its extremities), succeeds in maintaining harmony with its neighbours.

Designed and built with a blunt horizontal edge to its silhouette, this changed once the building was completed. In the nervous climate of the time, following a query from the powers that be as to whether a spire

V G Gelfreikh, M A Minkus 1948–53

Around the Garden Ring

V G Gelfreikh, M A Minkus 1948–53

was planned, a metal spire, coloured to imitate the stone below, was quickly added. This addition changed the perception of the whole square but connected the building with the silhouette of the other Stalin towers.

The main entrance on to the square carries obvious features of post-war classicism, visible in elements such as the decorative plasterwork of the three portals and the fitted metal grilles. The splendid and luxurious interiors, individually decorated with integral architectural ornament in expensive stones and metals, possess a lucidity resulting from the absence of any additional works of art.

Around the Garden Ring

ADDRESS Smolenskaya-Sennaya Ploshchad, 32–34
ENGINEER G Limanovsky
METRO Smolenskaya

V G Gelfreikh, M A Minkus 1948–53

V G Gelfreikh, M A Minkus 1948–53

Melnikov house

Among the most original examples of 20th-century architecture is this private house, created by one of its most talented and innovative exponents, Konstantin Stepanovich Melnikov. From its completion in 1929 to this day it has been the home of the Melnikov family.

This is a unique jewel of a building. Set back from its neighbours, it occupies a small plot of land in the city centre, in a small quiet lane between the new and the old Arbat. The building consists of two intersecting cylinders of equal diameter but different heights. The lower almost solid walled cylinder is cut by a flat vertical plane of glazing parallel to the street. One is not immediately aware of the second higher cylinder with its ornate pattern of hexagonal windows to the rear.

In a building of such strong geometric shapes the interior can often be compromised, but in this extraordinary home the interior spaces give no indication of the rigid external geometry. Such was Melnikov's genius that it seems as though the house has been designed from the inside out. The stunning yet comfortable living spaces were the result of his many years of experimentation and the evolution of his ideas on a place to live.

The entrance level includes the hall, dining room, kitchen, bathroom, utility, children's room and access to basement. On the second floor is the large double-height living room with a full-height window facing the street. At the rear of the floor above, a studio of the same size and shape is lit by a patterned wall of hexagonal windows. The different treatment of the fenestration in these areas – and the resultant quality of light – creates the perception of two totally different living spaces.

At the top of the stairs a door dividing the living room from the sleeping area to the rear is hinged in such a way that the stairs can lead directly into either room. Intriguing sleeping arrangements were created by means of two radial freestanding walls which form three wedge-shaped sleeping

K S Melnikov 1927–29

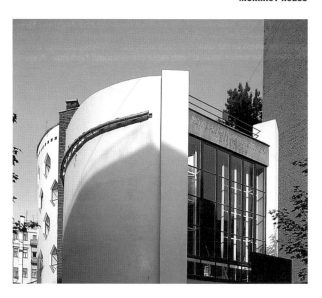

K S Melnikov 1927–29

areas, one for the parents and one each for their son and daughter. Originally, beds on fixed moulded and rendered bases were the sole furnishings, positioned in the centre of each area, but following damage during the war these were replaced with more conventional furniture. A spiral staircase leads to the studio and a further small mezzanine overlooks the main workspace and leads to a roof terrace over the living room.

As well as exploring the possibilities of form, space and light, Melnikov also employed an original method of construction using a traditional palette of materials. The external walls of the cylinders are built of brick in diagonal frames forming cells. This structural framework was then either filled with bricks or left to form the basis of diamond-shaped window openings. The floor structure is also cellular, with intersecting floor planks forming squares.

In the 1980s Melnikov's son Viktor started to restore the house, adamant that the integrity and techniques of the original be followed absolutely. His concern that this was not happening resulted in a disruption of the reconstruction, but work has since resumed and nears completion. Thanks to Viktor's love, tenacity and pride in his father's rare gift, the house will continue to be enjoyed by future generations.

ADDRESS Krivoarbatsky Pereulok, 10
METRO Arbatskaya

K S Melnikov 1927–29

K S Melnikov 1927–29

The White House

Following international news coverage of the August 1991 coup, The White House (Beli Dom) became familiar world wide as the backdrop to Yeltsin's famous speech from the top of a Soviet tank. In October 1993 it was again in the headlines, this time under siege, its windows blasted out and the white marble façade streaked black. The building was restored in 1994 following damage caused by shells from Russian tanks.

The 20-storey Russian Government building (previously the House of Soviets) is situated on a curve of the Moskva river. Its massive volume, a strictly symmetrical tiered form, is similar to that of projects in the 1930s by the same architects. Heavy and pompous, the granite-faced base looks particularly out of date, its wide steps leading from the embankment to the front entrance a reminder of the aesthetics of Stalinist classicism. Since the events of the early 1990s, this relationship with the river has changed: now a monumental ironwork fence separates the building from the embankment.

The centre of the composition is highlighted by a clock-tower decorated with a gold emblem of Russia and the state flag. The building is divided into two main parts: a lower seven-storey volume with side wings, and a central 20-storey section crowned with a band of narrow vertical windows surrounding the top technical floor. A wide selection of materials from all over the Russian Federation was used in the decoration of the House of Soviets. The white marble facing, garish against the predominantly muted tones of the city, is more appealing in the snow, when, on sunny days, it takes on the appearance of an exhibit from Moscow's annual international ice sculpture competition.

ADDRESS Krasnopresnenskaya Naberzhnaya, 2
METRO Krasnopresnenskaya, Barrikadnaya

Around the Garden Ring

D N Chechulin, P P Shteller and others 1965–81

D N Chechulin, P P Shteller and others 1965–81

The Ukraine Hotel

Positioned to dominate a sharp bend in the Moskva river is the least attractive of the seven Stalin towers, a 29-storey hotel reaching 170 metres in height, including the mandatory tower. In this cumbersome-looking building the architect's use of classicism is very much at variance with the non-traditional volumes and proportions of the structure, resulting in a harsh and incongruous silhouette.

The tower occupies a very important site at the start of Kutuzovsky Prospekt, with its main façade facing the river and the city centre, closing the perspective across the bridge as one approaches from the Novy Arbat. The White House and other large-scale developments came later, taking the Ukraine Hotel as the starting point in their development. Apart from 1000 hotel rooms, a restaurant and café, the multi-functional complex includes 254 apartments and several ground-floor shops.

Stylistically the hotel is a creation of Stalinist classicism. Its stunted tiers are crowned with massive sculptural decorations – pyramidal obelisks, Soviet five-ended stars and vases shaped as sheaves of wheat (the symbol of the Ukraine). Views of The White House above these ornaments are frequently used as the background for television news reports.

The atmosphere inside is distinctly Soviet: as well as the many elements of original decoration and furniture, the colours, lighting and smells are evocative of an era not long past.

ADDRESS Kutuzovsky Prospekt, 2/1
ASSOCIATED ARCHITECTS V K Oltarzhevsky, V G Kalish
ENGINEER P A Krasilnikov
METRO Kievskaya

A G Mordvinov 1950–56

Around the Garden Ring

A G Mordvinov 1950–56

Narkomfin apartments

Located on a large parkland site, the Narkomfin building originally enjoyed clear views to the Moskva river below. The site is now much reduced and encroached on by development on all sides – a sad monument to the ideals of collective living as expressed by Moisei Ginzburg and Ignaty Milinis. Recognised as one of the finest built examples of the constructivist rationalist aesthetic, it is now in an appalling condition – but although derelict in appearance, is still home to more than 20 families.

The Narkomfin was one of only six experimental residential buildings of this type built in the Soviet Union, in the cities of Moscow, Ekaterinburg and Saratov. These passage-type or transitional houses were based on the concept of the 'full collectivisation' of living, a scientific approach that required the restructuring of daily life. However, this approach proved unworkable, and was discontinued following its denouncement in 1930 by the Central Committee of the workers' party.

Research in the field of communal living was led by Ginzburg, who designed the best built example of this housing type. Constructed behind Moscow's Garden Ring on Tchaikovskova Ulitsa and designed for 50 families of the People's Commissariat for Finance, the complex was to have consisted of four blocks: a long six-storey residential building connected by a heated covered passageway to a four-storey cube housing a communal gymnasium and kitchen; a services block (only partly built) and a separate kindergarten (which was never realised). The kindergarten was eventually incorporated in the communal block, with the gymnasium excluded.

The main six-storey volume was raised on circular concrete columns, visually lifting the building and giving the impression that it is sitting in the centre of a green area. This, combined with the horizontal emphasis of the elevation, semi-circular balconies at one end and a two-level roof

M Y Ginzburg, I Milinis 1928–30

M Y Ginzburg, I Milinis 1928–30

Around the Garden Ring

garden, creates a vivid image of an ocean liner. Unfortunately the ground floor has now been closed in, detracting from the original effect. The entire composition has a strong Le Corbusier influence – which may well have been reciprocal. Le Corbusier asked Ginzburg for copies of the layouts of the apartments, which he then took back to Paris.

The apartments, cleverly designed as a series of different-sized duplex units, required only two of the six levels to have access corridors. Double-height living quarters were large and spacious, contrasting with the mean fragmented spaces allocated to service areas such as kitchens (residents were expected to use the communal services). In all aspects of the building, contrasts are the basis of the design. The strong horizontal bands of windows and balconies of the main building are broken by the animated outlines of the superstructures on the flat roof, both of which contradict the volume and pattern of the solid-cube community building with its modular glass-block north elevation.

The innovative ideas incorporated in the design of this building had a wide influence on both Soviet and foreign architecture.

Though an architectural masterpiece and a unique example of post-revolutionary ideology, this building proved a social disaster. After only a short time it was altered internally by its residents, who rejected the life-style it imposed. In spite of these alterations, the building's unique spatial qualities are still apparent today.

ADDRESS Tchaikovskova Ulitsa
ENGINEER S L Prohorov
METRO Barrikadnaya

M Y Ginzburg, I Milinis 1928–30

M Y Ginzburg, I Milinis 1928–30

Vosstaniya apartment building and gastronoms

Situated along the Garden Ring is another of the seven high-rise Stalin towers, a 160-metre-high, 22-storey central block flanked by 18-storey wings, laid out in an H-shaped plan. In 1950, when all seven were under construction, their impact on the city panorama was analysed. Subsequently, spires were added to the Lomonos State University (page 248), MID (page 126) and this tower (during the Soviet period its address was Vosstaniya Ploshchad).

In front of the building is a formal park; this sets the complex back from the busy Garden Ring and creates a sense of arrival when approaching from this road or the radial streets opposite. The wings of the buildings rise in terraces towards the central form, above which soars an octagonal tower dominating the nearby zoo and the Krasno Presnensky region, both situated on low-lying ground. The stepping-down of the wings at the sides also reduces the scale in keeping with its surroundings.

To the right (north side) of the tower is Vdovy (widow's) house. This famous classical two-storey almshouse was designed in 1775 by Giovany Batista Jelardy and, following a fire, was reconstructed by his son Dominic. On the opposite southern boundary of the square a new hotel and business centre is under construction, intended to counterbalance the overall composition. That project is under the direction of M M Posokhin, son of one of the original architects of the Vosstaniya building.

The rough-cut granite-faced stylobate on which the building rests forms a terrace for promenading, and accommodates shops below (previously there was also a children's cinema called Barrikady). The main façades are all divided by pilasters which, running full height, underline the vertical emphasis of the building. Decorated with allegorical sculp-

M V Posokhin, A A Mndoyants 1950–54

M V Posokhin, A A Mndoyants 1950–54

tures, reliefs, and architectural motifs borrowed from Moscow architecture of the Naryshkinsky style, they demonstrate the orientation towards nationalist tradition prevalent in post-war Soviet architecture.

Residents have been cautious about undertaking invasive construction work on the fabric of this building – and with good reason. Convicts were used in the construction of this and many other buildings in the capital. It is said that on this site one particularly cruel foreman threw a convict into the still-wet concrete, where it is assumed he remains to this day.

In addition to 452 apartments, the building also included four food halls, each called Gastronom. They occupied the four outer corners of the complex at podium level, and each supplied specific food stuffs such as dairy produce, meat or fish. The palatial interiors of these halls were unrivalled examples of the rich decoration of the Stalinist classical style.

On the western corner, the recent Le Gastronom restaurant occupies the former fish hall, maintaining much of its sumptuous interior. Tall square white marbled columns topped with white and gold ceramic Corinthian details draw one's eye to the high coffered ceilings. At floor level the columns formerly separated the white-marble-topped serving counters which stood between them on a geometrically patterned stone floor. Behind the counters, recesses which previously held large decorative urns now contrast with red marbled walls, and above them the original stained-glass panels still depict colourful images of fish. Only the abacus appears to be missing, replaced by electronic tills.

ADDRESS Kudrinskaya Ploshchad
ENGINEER M N Vokhomsky
METRO Barrikadnaya

M V Posokhin, A A Mndoyants 1950–54

M V Posokhin, A A Mndoyants 1950–54

House of the Ex-Political (Tsarist) Prisoners Society

Only a section of the original project was ever realised, including the club/theatre facilities intended as the nucleus of the complex. An additional planned museum was not built. In 1934 the club was disbanded, at a time when its name, following the first of the Stalinist purges, would have taken on a somewhat different meaning. Later, the building became The Theatre for Film Actors, the only theatre in the world specifically intended for film actors to perform when not otherwise employed.

To differentiate this development from their other constructivist work, it had been the Vesnin brothers' intention to hang panels of decorative relief over the main entrance, though this was never carried out. But even in its truncated form the impressive plasticity of the intersecting volumes is evident, combining smooth concrete walls and corner glazing. Overall it is one of the most interesting and one of the last examples of constructivist architecture. The club represents a proportionally exact asymmetrical composition, with an elegant external staircase leading to the main entrance. One needs to avert one's eyes to avoid the recent shameful addition of a brick lean-to entrance tucked in a corner at ground level, but not so easy to obliterate are the ubiquitous kiosks which litter the edges of the small green park on the previously open external corner of the site.

The commodious internal volumes reflect the simplicity of the exterior in the spacious audience hall and colourful foyer with its large windows.

Of literary interest is the period residence across the road, appropriately occupied by the Union of Writers. It features in Tolstoy's *War and Peace* as Dom Rostovikh, the fictitious home of the novel's hero.

ADDRESS Povarskaya Ulitsa, 33
METRO Krasnopresnenskaya, Barrikadnaya

V A, A A and L A Vesnin 1929–34

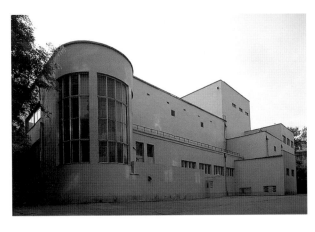

V A, A A and L A Vesnin 1929–34

School No. 20 extension

Identified by number, as was standard during the Soviet period, this élite English-language school for Russians is in an old neighbourhood of predominantly 19th-century residential buildings. The relatively small scale of this project, satisfying a basic brief for additional classrooms and recreational facilities, belies its complexity. Situated between two perpendicular buildings (a 19th-century mansion and a standard Soviet post-Second World War school building), the school presented a further challenge in that its site was visibly open to Shchuseva Ulitsa, directly backing on to a building occupied by the Russian Union of Architects.

A large four-storey curved volume unites the two existing buildings. The apparent simplicity of the solution clearly demonstrates both Asadov's talent and his design philosophy. Like many of his colleagues, he opposes the 'dictatorship of right-angled forms in architecture'; he also likes to create contrasts by using curved and circular architectural solutions to articulate contemporary interventions within earlier structures.

Expressively determined and bridging the two architecturally diverse existing buildings, the curved extension relates more closely to the rationalist aesthetic of the school building, discernible in the solution of the curved rendered façade with its almost regular rhythm of fenestration. Set back from the solid four-storey façade and expressed as a fifth floor is a totally glazed tower-like structure providing natural light for the double-height recreational hall below. The extension's relationship to the mansion is more complex, picking up on its terracotta colour, the proportions of its regular two-storey façade, and its classical-style cornice detail.

ADDRESS Vspolnii Pereulok, 6
ENGINEERS S F Churikov, E A Kondratev
METRO Barrikadnaya

A P Asadov, E I Chastnova 1995

A P Asadov, E I Chastnova 1995

Planetarium

The gates to this provocative design are set back from the Garden Ring. Once the gates have been unlocked, one approaches the building down a tree- and sculpture-lined avenue. Through the gap in the trees along the central path the egg-shaped silver dome of the main hall peeps through invitingly.

This constructivist building brought fame to its two young architects for their introduction of a new type of institution within a novel building type. It was the first scientific building in the USSR designed not only for scientific purposes but also for the entertainment of the people. Alexei Gan, the ideologist of constructivism, described it as 'a theatre without actors in which men served science by presenting it optically with the aid of complicated equipment'.

The core of the building, situated on the second floor, is a round hall seating 500. This is roofed with a reinforced-concrete parabolic cupola, 12 centimetres thick at its foot, reducing to 8 centimetres at its upper part. As the authors had intended, the silvery cupola was perceived as a symbol of technical and scientific progress. (Similar metallic imagery was to appear on many later scientific buildings.) The main cupola of the building is extended by simply formed rectangular service extensions. The entrance area was reconstructed at a later stage.

The planetarium has been closed for some years and is currently undergoing reconstruction.

ADDRESS Sadovaya-Kudrinskaya Ulitsa, 5
RECONSTRUCTION A P Asadov, A Chastnov, A V Anisimov (adviser)
METRO Barrikadnaya, Krasnopresnenskaya

M O Barshch, M I Sinyavsky (original) 1927–29

M O Barshch, M I Sinyavsky (original) 1927–29

Around the Garden Ring

Administration building

The area behind the north side of Mayakovskaya Ploshchad is dominated by multi-storey administrative buildings, a number of which are the offices of huge State architectural institutions. These Mosproekts employ thousands of architects and are individually identified by number, as are their subdivisions, which are called Masterskayas (studios).

When Mosproekt 1 (Studio 2) was developing this architectural composition, their main objective was to treat the building as a consummate piece of art – an objective they successfully accomplished in this attractively articulated building, its expression still modern and undated.

Situated on a corner site, the stocky block has a sculptural quality, achieved by a combination of curves and deep recesses which break up the large brick surfaces. Alternative treatments on the flat brick walls create a richness with complex and harmonious rhythms that are both static and dynamic.

As well as giving this building a strong individual identity, the architects have also preserved the harmony of the existing area by using traditional features characteristic of this part of the city.

Around the Garden Ring

ADDRESS 1st Brestskaya Ulitsa, 4–6/Tverskaya Ulitsa, 33–35
ENGINEERS A L Gordon, B N Lyashovsky, V A Strizhachenko
METRO Mayakovskaya

Mosproekt 1 (Studio 2): M K Bylinkin, A Meerson, A V Repety 1965

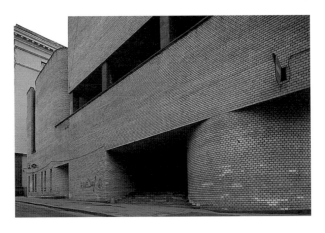

Mosproekt 1 (Studio 2): M K Bylinkin, A Meerson, A V Repety 1965

Apartment building

This fine house in the classical Stalinist style occupies the entire block between Blagoveshchensky and Mamonovsky lanes. Although its volume is pretty ordinary, the proportions and execution of décor are very elegant. The blocks were built in two stages, connected by a slightly recessed three-level arcade with a shallow curved roof. Both parts of the building have different details, cornice patterns and window sizes, yet achieve a completeness as one architectural ensemble. On the left side of the building is one of the first examples of the use of classical elements in residential architecture. To enrich the façade, the architect incorporated inserts of scratch-work technique, an innovative first step towards the synthesis of architecture and fine art.

It is interesting to compare this restrained classical approach, very much dictated by the restraints of the location, with the concrete-panelled apartment building by Burov on Leningradsky Prospekt (the Azhurny apartment building; see page 232) which, although a totally different architectural solution, also combines art and architecture in expressive decorative panels.

see page 232

Around the Garden Ring

ADDRESS Tverskaya Ulitsa, 25
ARTIST V Favorsky
METRO Mayakovskaya, Pushkinskaya

A K Burov 1933–36, 1949

A K Burov 1933–36, 1949

Unikom bank

Situated down a lane in a predominantly business area of the city, the Unikom bank towers over its modest uninspiring neighbours. The heavy cubic mass of this grey stone and glass building is fractured by triangular prisms of glass which pierce the walls and roof. This manner is continued in the design of the separate structure of the glass porch. Set back from the street line, the building was originally open to the street but now, presumably in the interests of security, it is enclosed behind perimeter metal fencing. Although attractively detailed, the sculptural quality of the bank is masked by this outer screen which affects one's perception of the building within the site.

The interior has been cleverly designed to form a variety of internal volumes. From the glazed porch corner entrance, the directional path continues through the building volume, dissecting it diagonally with a narrow full-height atrium. The bank's forceful dynamism and unusual spatial form are reminiscent of Melnikov's USSR Pavilion at the 1925 International Exhibition in Paris (a rectangular pavilion divided by a wide staircase cutting diagonally through its length).

The atrium path is suspended over the first basement level, with large triangular light wells either side creating double-height spaces and a bright open atmosphere. The cube and square are used as decorative elements and can be seen in the stone floor pattern, in the open steel structure to the roof above the atrium, and in its suspended light fittings.

ADDRESS Daev Pereulok
ARCHITECTS D Solopov, L Altabayeva, L Ivanova, V Kolosnitsin, D Pshenichnikov; Firm AMR (Austria): G Korsdorf
ENGINEER A Plax
METRO Sukharevskaya

Around the Garden Ring

Mosproekt 2 (Studio 2) 1996

Narkomzem building

This dynamic building for the Commissariat (Ministry) of Agriculture has a memorable volumetric composition and is an outstanding creation of late constructivism. Alexei Shchusev – far from a proponent of constructivism in his creative aspirations – demonstrates here the full range of his architectural diversity. The building is beautifully articulated using elements characteristic of the constructivist approach – ribbon windows, smooth curved corners, asymmetry, intercrossing volumes – to create a wholesome and expressive image.

A nine-storey, concrete-framed and curtain-walled structure with outer elevations facing on to three streets, the building surrounds a quadrilateral inner court. Shchusev has exploited the opportunities offered by curtain walling in his plastic use of both glass and render. The pinky brown render was intended to resemble the tuff volcanic stone used on Le Corbusier's nearby Tsentrosoyuz (page 106), and in fact this imitation has aged more attractively than its natural counterpart.

Shchusev's approach to the interior design maintains the clarity and integrity characteristic of the building envelope.

ADDRESS Sadovaya-Spasskaya Ulitsa, 11–13
ASSOCIATED ARCHITECTS D D Bulgankov, I A Frantsuz, G K Yakovlev
METRO Krasniye Vorota

A V Shchusev 1929–33

A V Shchusev 1929–33

Gostorg (Ministry of Trade)

Designed as the headquarters of the Ministry of Trade, this early example of constructivism is composed of a number of symmetrically placed interconnected blocks, their juxtaposition creating two inner courtyards. The original design included a 14-storey tower in the centre, but this was never realised.

Manifesting constructivist ideology, the treatment of the façades is crisp and unembellished. The reinforced-concrete structure is clearly visible, both where it divides the steel-framed glazing and where the horizontal bands of glass cross in front of the vertical elements and wrap around the corners of the structure.

The large areas of glazing provided good natural lighting to the vestibules, cafeterias, lower-level service spaces and offices above, but also produced thermal problems, prompting office personnel to switch from one side of the building to the other according to the prevailing weather conditions.

Le Corbusier, whose Tsentrosoyuz complex is situated nearby, is said to have described this building as 'an ideal vertical beehive'. (Velikovsky, together with V M Voinov, was the architect of the winning entry for the open competition for the Tsentrosoyuz building in 1928. Le Corbusier was awarded the commission after participation in a subsequent closed competition.)

ADDRESS Myasnitskaya Ulitsa, 47
METRO Krasniye Vorota

B M Velikovsky/A Y Langman, M O Barshch et al 1925–27

Around the Garden Ring

B M Velikovsky/A Y Langman, M O Barshch et al 1925–27

Lermontov Tower

This 24-storey residential and administrative skyscraper is set in the midst of several interesting constructivist buildings, including the Krasniye Vorota metro station directly opposite on the other side of the Garden Ring. The site was previously occupied by the residence where the great Russian poet M Lermontov was born. In the internal yard to the rear of the high-rise structure there is a monument to him created by the artist Brodsky.

Like the other Stalin skyscrapers, this one is executed in the style of Soviet neo-classicism. Enriched by decorative motifs, it is closer in architectural principle to the tiered buildings of old Russia than the other Stalin towers, though compositionally it is less interesting.

The taller central block housing the offices of the Ministry for Transport Machinery is crowned by an elegant spire and flanked by two lower residential blocks. The vertical accent is stressed in the treatment of the lower façade, which is divided by flat stone pilasters crossing the dark horizontal tiers. The central axis of the building is emphasised by a sculptural coat of arms of the former Soviet Union in stone.

The tower contains an entrance to I A Fomin's Krasnye Vorota metro station, over which the building stands. The beautiful interiors of the underground hall and overground vestibule of this station are decorated in natural stone and fine plaster work (see pages 290 and 292).

ADDRESS Lermontovskaya Ploshchad, 21
ENGINEER V Abramov
METRO Krasniye Vorota

A N Dushkin, B S Mezentsev 1949–53

A N Dushkin, B S Mezentsev 1949–53

Leningradskaya Hotel

Overlooking three major railway stations is the smallest of the seven Stalin towers, the Leningradskaya Hotel. At 17 storeys high, it also serves as a vertical landmark identifying the transport hub of the city. Originally the tower terminated the view from Komsomolskaya Ploshchad, with Leningradsky, Yaroslavsky and Kazansky railway stations to the left and right, but the panorama is now shortened by a railway bridge which runs right in front of the tower. This effectively cuts the hotel off, leaving the neat rectangular building on a virtual traffic island in a no man's land of cars and trains.

In an effort to communicate harmoniously with the diverse styles of its neighbours – 19th- and early 20th-century railway buildings by architects Ton, Shekhtel and Shchusev – the hotel's repetitive stone-clad façades are ornamented with stylised motifs taken from 18th-century Russian architecture.

As a contrast to the relatively ordered exterior, the lavish interior is well worth a look. It exhibits a variety of decorative elements, but gothic motifs predominate, adorning items such as doors and tiered ecclesiastical chandeliers. In the heavily marbled main entrance hall, green freestanding circular columns support a heavily gilded coffered ceiling, while a pair of pale marble staircases lead off to the left and right, emphasising the impressive double height of the space.

ADDRESS Kalanchevskaya Ulitsa, 21–40
ENGINEER Y Metlyuk
METRO Prospekt Mira, Komsomolskaya

L M Polyakov, A B Boretsky, A S Rochegov 1949–53

L M Polyakov, A B Boretsky, A S Rochegov 1949–53

Clinic for the Ministry of Transport

Fomin, as main architect for the Ministry of Transport, executed three projects in the immediate Krasnye Vorota area. All designed and executed in the final years of his life, their architectural diversity illustrates Fomin's proletarian classicism. Unlike Zholtovsky's strict and exact replications of classicism (see page 36), this interpretative approach used classical elements as an architectural language which allowed for creative intuition in their application.

The clinic is arranged in three perpendicular blocks and is situated across the road from Fomin's offices for the same client (page 168) and the Stalin tower above his Krasnye Vorota metro station (see page 162). The regular pink-rendered façade of this harmonious composition exhibits a conservative restraint, enlivened by a simple single-storey colonnade. Contained at the extremities, the open walkway forms a two-sided courtyard to the front of the clinic.

Solid horizontal rendered bands between the floors and the clear structural module dividing the fenestration lend the façades an almost industrial aesthetic. Softened by form and massing, this individualism is further expressed in the unusual plan: two curved ends at the extremities of the building turn in towards each other, creating a dynamic compositional form. This unusual massing is also found in Fomin's Dinamo building for the KGB (see page 48).

The clinic was started in 1932 and completed after Fomin's death by N S Petrov, in accordance with the original drawings.

ADDRESS Novaya Basmannaya Ulitsa, 5
METRO Krasniye Vorota

I A Fomin, N S Petrov 1932–36

I A Fomin, N S Petrov 1932–36

MPS (Ministry of Transport)

This modernist envelope – in an even more palpable constructivist spirit than the polyclinic (see page 166) – resulted from the reconstruction of an 18th-century auxiliary building called the Empress Palace (although it was actually used to store provisions). At the turn of the century it had been renovated and extended by the Institute of Moscow Nobility – for what was to be only a brief occupancy – and in 1918, after the revolution, it was taken over by the Ministry of Transport.

The building was radically changed after Fomin's intervention. The focal point of the grey rendered ensemble is now a corner clock tower which terminates the perspective along the Garden Ring. The vertical emphasis of the tower is reiterated in a continuous vertical band of glazing and the asymmetrically spaced elongated columns below.

Fomin's characteristic attenuated half columns without bases or capitals echo the rhythm of the original palace fenestration and give the building a captivating liveliness. On the south, Sadovaya façade is an opening for vehicles. At this point the columns become three dimensional, producing the effect of raising the building on legs.

The constructivist language of Fomin's design is intriguing, as the popularity of unadorned functionalism was waning. This building is different too from his polyclinic opposite and the nearby Krasnye Vorota metro underground hall (see page 292), which more closely reflect his proletarian classicism.

ADDRESS Sadovaya/Chernogryazskaya Ulitsa, 1
METRO Krasniye Vorota

I A Fomin 1930–34

I A Fomin 1930–34

Taganka and Zamoskvorechye

Kotelniki apartment building

This residential building on the embankment down from the Hotel Russia is at the point where the Moskva and Yauza rivers join (where an eighth, unrealised, Stalin Tower had been planned), terminating the perspective of the streets leading down to the river from the Kremlin. Dominating the whole district, its singular silhouette in the hook of the river hides the panorama of the Shvivaya Gorka (one of Moscow's seven hills), a picturesque view previously enjoyed from the city centre.

The footprint of the 24-storey central tower (a three-rayed plan) gradually increases in scale, from a relationship with the low surrounding area at its extremities, up to the central apex. The impressive silhouette of the central volume, flanked by three lower towers, extends beyond the trefoil with further side wings along the two rivers.

Faced in a rusticated warm red granite, the five lower floors define the base of the building; intermediate levels change to a light stone finish, while the tops of the lower towers and the 176-metre-high central apex are crowned in a light render. Over-sized obelisks, statues and other elements of heavy decoration create an unbalanced composition, and yet the overall effect is harmonious.

These high-quality, high-ceilinged apartments for the privileged, finished in marble, steel and hardwood, with stunning views of the river and Kremlin, can often be spotted in the background of classic black-and-white Soviet films. Accommodation in the complex also includes car parking, shops and The Illusion cinema – in Soviet times the only one in Moscow showing undubbed foreign films.

ADDRESS Zvonarsky Pereulok, 5
ENGINEER V A Platonov
METRO Kuznetsky Most

Taganka and Zamoskvorechye

D N Chechulin, A K Rostkovsky 1948–52

D N Chechulin, A K Rostkovsky 1948–52

Taganka drama and comedy theatre

Founded in 1964 by internationally famous producer Yuri Lubimov and D Borovsky, the theatre takes its name from the old marketing district in which it is located. This innovative complex, an exciting penetration of unique volumes, is intertwined with restored and expanded old structures, including an original theatre building. The new parts of the complex, finished both externally and internally in red brick with highlighted limestone details, reflect the colours of the 17th-century Nikola church directly opposite. In sharp contrast, the existing 19th- and early 20th-century structures, though integrated into the mass of the new composition, maintain their identity with their original bright stucco façades.

The architects have cleverly used the potential problem of a 6-metre drop at the rear of the steeply sloping site to resolve the difficult organisation of the backstage areas. Huge blank planes of brick protect the magical, theatrical world within from the noise and distraction of the nearby highway. Reducing in scale from the rear of the complex, the brick-clad volumes culminate in a low heavy horizontal band of brick overhanging the deep-set theatre entrance.

As one looks into the interior from the main entrance, visible beyond the foyer is a landscaped open courtyard, the core of the whole composition. This triangular well of light seems particularly vibrant against the predominantly brick interior.

Parts of the restored historical buildings are used as performance halls seating up to 500 people; other facilities also include a theatre café, bar and staff rooms.

The architects' primary spatial concept for the interior required that any areas where people gather, in addition to their normal function, should be useable as performance space. This flexibility has been

A V Anisimov, Y P Gnedovsky, B I Tarantsev 1973–85

A V Anisimov, Y P Gnedovsky, B I Tarantsev 1973–85

achieved, but I am unsure if it is actually exploited. The new hall, which seats 750, has the ability to metamorphose, providing transformable performance space (a requirement of theatres in the 1980s).

Entertainment takes on a whole new meaning in this amazing theatre, a result of the combined creative genius of Lubimov and Gnedovsky. Features include a central stage supplemented by side wings, with the left side separated from the audience by a flexible, movable screen. On the right, the backdrop can literally be the Moscow cityscape, seen through a 10-by-4.5-metre opening, revealed by lowering a moveable reinforced-concrete wall. Connected by external stairs to the street, it also provides an interesting point of arrival for performers. Another unique element is the back wall of the centre-stage area. This freestanding wall, the brick façade of an earlier building, has stairs and shutters constructed behind it, allowing access. Wonderful dramatic effects are created using the three levels of window openings.

Although pioneering in its technical and theatrical innovations, the strongest abiding memory of this complex is its architectural solution. With its sculptural and expressive silhouette, the theatre is a stylistically unified composition; one's impressions change dramatically as one moves around and through this memorable architectural ensemble.

ADDRESS Verchnyaya Radishshevskaya Ulitsa, 19/3
ENGINEERS V Berlitsky, I Gerasimov
METRO Taganskaya

A V Anisimov, Y P Gnedovsky, B I Tarantsev 1973–85

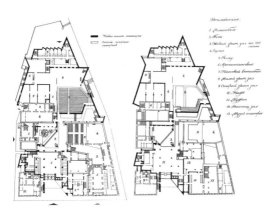

A V Anisimov, Y P Gnedovsky, B I Tarantsev 1973–85

Mosenka Park towers

When looking at this building one needs yet again to consider the built architecture in terms of what was originally intended. In a sad reflection of the difficulties experienced by those struggling to realise innovative developments at this time, the architects are 'relatively satisfied' with the result in that the volume and spatial composition of the project are more or less as they intended. The complex was to have included apartments, but as a result of market conditions it is entirely commercial– 25,000 square metres of office space and underground car parking.

Printed shades of grey cannot convey the impression this building makes. Behind the 'reconstructed' highly decorative and colourful two-storey 19th-century façades along the existing street line, bursts an unworldly elliptical mass, its swollen bulk towering over the neighbouring park. With its alternating bands of glass and bright-yellow panels, it has all the elegance of a Sumo wrestler in a tight football jersey. Sensibly designed in light blue, the panel colour was changed in an effort to realise the project, blue not being a favorite with the decision makers.

Towering behind the staggered horizontal bands of the nine-storey mass are two 13-storey towers. Their height, façade alignment and alternative fenestration relate strongly to and cleverly continue the rhythm of the adjoining apartment blocks. Here at least one can clearly appreciate the architects' skill.

ADDRESS Taganskaya Ulitsa, 17–23
ARCHITECTS S B Tkachenko, O L Dubrovsky, T I Reves, I M Dolinskaya, N A Shabelnikova
ENGINEERS V A Gnedin, Y V Skachkova
METRO Taganskaya, Marksistskaya

Mosproekt 2 (Studio 15) 1996

Taganka and Zamoskvorechye

Taganka and Zamoskvorechye

Mosproekt 2 (Studio 15) 1996

ZIL cultural palace

By the early 1930s, workers' clubs, referred to as 'cultural palaces', had increased in scale, as individual facilities for each enterprise were superseded by larger centres catering for groups of enterprises or entire urban districts. In contrast to the earlier single-volume solutions explored by Melnikov and others, these sizeable social centres allowed for the breakdown of the building mass into multiple components.

The Vesnin brothers were commissioned to design this palace by the union of steelworkers, together with the workers of the industrial enterprises of the Proletarsky district. Their commission followed a design competition which had attracted great interest; it was seen to mark an important stage in the rivalry between architectural styles, and teams representing all the architectural associations participated. Unsurprisingly, as Alexander Vesnin, the leader of constructivism, was one of its authors, the realised design is one of the best examples of this building type. Featuring a favourite constructivist device – pavilions linked by passages – the resulting creation is a harmonious assembly of components in unison with the surrounding landscape.

The complex was designed as three main blocks – a club house and two theatres – but with political trends moving away from the construction of large halls, the dominant 4000-seat auditorium was never built. Without it, the interaction and orientation of the building mass were changed, resulting in a neutral elevation to the street, with the main axis of the building relating to the park gardens at the side and rear. The clubhouse accommodation, T-shaped in plan, includes a 1000-seat auditorium, library, winter garden, observatory, and restaurant at ground-floor level. A staircase to the second floor overlooks the projecting semicircular winter garden and the banks of the Moskva river beyond.

The club (more recently known as the ZIL Club, after the nearby car

Taganka and Zamoskvorechye

V A and A A Vesnin 1931–37

Taganka and Zamoskvorechye

V A and A A Vesnin 1931–37

plant) is still an enjoyable place of social interaction, and its bright interior spaces have a pleasant relaxed atmosphere. On my recent visit, a well-attended ballroom dancing class, half-watched by those relaxing nearby, was being held in the columned second-floor exhibition hall which connects through to the theatre foyer.

Part of the club's parkland site was formerly occupied by the Simonov monastery, much of which was blown up to make room for this Soviet centre of congregation. The large site, as alternative schemes illustrated, could easily have accommodated both buildings. The needless destruction of the monastery – a redundant religious icon considered of no cultural value in an atheist society – is a reflection of the communist slogan 'culture instead of religion'.

Taganka and Zamoskvorechye

ADDRESS Vostochnaya Ulitsa, 4
METRO Proletarskaya, Avtozavodskaya

V A and A A Vesnin 1931–37

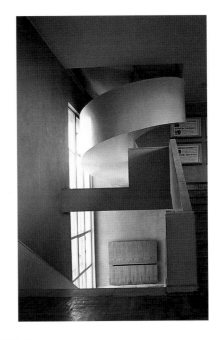

Taganka and Zamoskvorechye

V A and A A Vesnin 1931–37

Russian cultural centre

Down river from the ZIL Club, opposite the restored Novo Spasskii monastery, is one of the largest current developments in the city. On the arrow tip of the Kremlin island, this ambitious and innovative cultural centre combines social and architectural concepts in an expression that looks set to be unequivocally 20th-century Russian. Its important 7-hectare site along the river embankment was originally destined for a sports centre, but in the 1970s this scheme was superseded by a competition for a 'narodni dom' (people's palace).

In 1987 work began on the design of an international theatre complex (two of its authors, Yuri Gnedovsky and Vladilen Krasilnikov, are among the city's leading theatre experts). By the time construction started in 1995 this had become more of a mixed development, though a theatre remains one of the cultural elements to be included. To date commercial reality has resulted in the unusual pencil-shaped office blocks taking precedence, but one earnestly hopes the intended interesting mix of activities will survive. In addition to the completed commercial structures, internal and external cultural elements will mingle with cafés, shops, sports facilities and a hotel (soon to be under construction). This social, commercial and cultural mix, if successful, will result in both day and night activity within the complex, establishing a cohesive social nucleus and arts quarter currently lacking in the city. Although it is mainly an industrial and trade district, Zamoskvorechye (beyond the Moskva river) has been peppered with cultural establishments since the arrival of the Tretyakovskaya gallery at the end of the 19th century.

Another positive aspect of the centre's design is the manner in which it addresses the waterfront. Tiered terraces stepping down to the embankment and a pier where boats can stop off during the summer months will open up a welcome dialogue between the complex and the river. It is

Y Gnedovsky, V Krasilnikov, S Gnedovsky, M Gavrilova 1995–2000

Y Gnedovsky, V Krasilnikov, S Gnedovsky, M Gavrilova 1995–2000

hoped that a development of this type and scale, connected by pedestrian bridges and underground walkways to the surrounding district, will have a ripple effect beyond its boundaries, resulting in the regeneration of the local environment.

The design and composition of the completed corner of the site – composed of two small towers and a third block forming a perimeter wall along the canal – is plainly a witty modern reading of Kremlin and monastery traditions (vertical towers surrounded by fortified walls fixing and uniting the central elements). The architects have stated that their objective was to create a balance between a traditional and a modern approach which at the same time adds to the rich silhouette of the Moscow skyline. They intend to avoid any unity of materials, style, form, colour and scale between the individual blocks, though they will be in harmony with each other. Developing the complex in five stages may help the architects to achieve their aspiration.

ADDRESS Kosmodamianskaya Naberezhnaya/3rd Shlyuzovoy Pereulok
METRO Paveletskaya

Y Gnedovsky, V Krasilnikov, S Gnedovsky, M Gavrilova 1995–2000

Y Gnedovsky, V Krasilnikov, S Gnedovsky, M Gavrilova 1995–2000

Sachkredit bank

In the recently evolved market economy of the 1990s, bank buildings are a relatively new commodity. The Sachkredit bank represents a further new development, combining commercial and residential premises. Also novel is the rare opportunity afforded two young inexperienced architects (a group up until this time virtually confined to the realms of paper architecture) – the chance to construct a serious project. Constructed at a turning point in recent architectural developments, the resulting building vindicates the sage client's investment in previously uncharted waters. Though some details reflect the authors' lack of experience in understanding building materials and their application, they do not detract from the achievement of these talented architects.

The bank is situated in a residential area of the old city, on a quiet tree-lined street which still includes a number of merchants' mansions from previous centuries. The site of the proposed bank included one such residence and the new design was required to maintain its two-storey period façade. In an innovative manner, the three-storey semi-circular extension, considerably larger than the original, hides shyly behind the main façade. On approaching the building one is almost unaware of a new intervention, since only the third-floor pitched gable shows over the roof of the two-storey original.

Deception of scale is cleverly achieved by the curved walls of the extension: there is no side or back elevation and the new walls continue seamlessly from one original side elevation to the other. Equally skilfully handled is the division of the internal spaces.

ADDRESS Bakhrushina Ulitsa, 10
ENGINEER A Morozov
METRO Paveletskaya

Taganka and Zamoskvorechye

'Lara-Dit': D Dologoy, M Tovve 1991–93

'Lara-Dit': D Dologoy, M Tovve 1991–93

Office building

Taking a five-minute stroll down Bakhrushina Ulitsa towards Pavelet-skaya and a right turn on to 5th Monetchikovsky Pereulok, we come across another solution to the problem of extending and renovating. The architect's overall brief, from developer client J V Posad, was for a building achieving the maximum lettable area with the flexibility to meet the requirements of either a hoped-for bank client or, alternatively, multiple tenant occupancy. Town planning requirements again insisted on the restoration – or to be more accurate in this instance the 'rebuilding', as they had been destroyed in the 1970s – of two historical buildings on the site. Kisselev's solution treats the building as two separate parts. The new decorative three-storey block, set back from the two 'historical' structures, is embellished in a post-modernish dialogue which envelops them.

More successful – though its relationship to the other two parts seems to be ignored – is the modern block to the rear. Appearing more comfortable with a crisp modern almost industrial aesthetic in concrete and rendered brick, the attractive building is most enjoyed by the authors themselves, as their offices occupy part of the third floor and the glazed superstructure with barrelled roof above. An added bonus for the architects working in this busy practice are the summer parties on the extremely pleasant flat roof terrace.

ADDRESS 5th Monetchikovsky Pereulok, 38
ENGINEER I Shwartsman
METRO Paveletskaya

Taganka and Zamoskvorechye

Sergei Kisselev and Partners 1996

Sergei Kisselev and Partners 1996

Stolichny bank

One of the first new buildings in post-Soviet years to be designed and built by Western architects was this commercial structure commissioned by the Stolichny bank for its own use. Situated on a south-facing infill site on the embankment of the Vodootvodny canal, this subtle and enterprising solution is a response to an open brief and restrictive planning regulations (see also pages 188 and 190).

The low modest opening of the main entrance – an existing porch in the reconstructed period façade – increases in height to reveal the complete volume of the original solid structure, in contrast with the light steel and glass of the adjoining modern intervention. Beyond this intermediary space is the bright and spectacular central atrium. Under its dramatic curved glass roof, lightweight steel bridges connect the two blocks on either side. Animating this space is a suspended mobile by Georgy Frangulyan, its shining coin-shaped leaves a reminder of the main activities of the building. Competing for one's attention are the glass-screened lifts gliding elegantly between floors.

Integrated skilfully into the streetscape, the three-storey building increases in modernly articulated steps to five storeys at the rear of the deep site. The only disturbance to this comfortable integration is a solid gable emphasised by garish signage. Visible as one approaches along the Sadovnicheskaya Embankment from Paveletskaya, this gable was to have abutted a development intended to replace the neighbouring lower building, but which was unfortunately not realised.

ADDRESS Komissariatsky Most/Ozerkovskaya Naberezhnaya
ENGINEERS Ove Arup & Partners
METRO Novokuznetskaya

Murray O'Laoire International 1992–94

Taganka and Zamoskvorechye

Murray O'Laoire International 1992–94

'Electro Stantsiya No. 1' boiler house

This boiler house forms part of an industrial complex begun in 1896 as a station for the Electrical Lighting Society. In the 1920s, when several architects contributed to its development, it acquired various features of constructivism, including a seven-storey building on the embankment by V Dubovsky.

Throughout his life Zholtovsky remained a staunch traditionalist, tenacious in the practice and teaching of the classical style (see page 36). In the late 1920s he took a two-pronged approach against constructivism, relegating it to industrial buildings and harmonising its utilitarian forms. Here he explores the frontier between innovation and classicism, adding to the architectural forms of the boiler house a new tectonic expression in steel and glass while preserving the principles of harmonisation characteristic of classical architecture.

Now hidden behind solid high walls and security gates, the new glass wall faces on to a yard, its protruding, faceted oriole windows hidden from the view of ordinary mortals. Only from adjoining courtyards can one enjoy the upper levels of this plastically diverse building, unless one is lucky enough to be positioned near the solid gates as they open briefly to expel or ingest a vehicle. But even such a fleeting glimpse reveals broken windows and a general state of decay which may well be the reason for the secrecy surrounding this power station. Above a row of porthole windows, distinctive and tapering ship-like funnels – once black but now painted a less dramatic cream – announce this wonderful building above the rooftops.

ADDRESS Raushskaya Naberezhnaya
METRO Novokuznetskaya

Taganka and Zamoskvorechye

I V Zholtovsky 1929

Taganka and Zamoskvorechye

I V Zholtovsky 1929

North

Zuev club

Ilya Golosov was one of the most successful interpreters of constructivist methods in the 1920s. Although he experimented in different styles (and reverted to classicism when constructivism was condemned), his main interest was the spatial composition of buildings. Exploring the opportunities offered by constructivism, he achieved in the pure geometric forms of the Zuev club one of the most famous examples of the genre.

Developed on a small, difficult site, the compact rectangular mass of the building occupies 90 per cent of the available ground. Its most interesting aspect is the superb sculptural composition of the external volume, constructed in concrete, brick and glass. Original sketches of the club (for members of a tram depot) by Melnikov included a number of cylinders, their rationalist aesthetic intended to evoke associations with transport. In Golosov's realised design there is only one. On the corner of two streets the unusual, forceful form of his angular glass cylinder enclosing the staircase has a strong vertical presence, piercing through the rectangular concrete band of the third floor and continuing upwards until it is delicately contained by a thin rectangular plate.

The original club interior is now in a shabby condition and has unfortunately been altered. Its spacious double-height entrance foyer has been closed off to form an additional room, totally spoiling the original open approach. The luminous glass-block wall wrapping the circular staircase and the dynamic ceiling above beautifully demonstrate a pure constructivist aesthetic. At second-floor level directly above the stairs an expressive circular ceiling pattern is created by the concrete beam structure. Fluorescent tubes between each beam reiterate the radial movement.

ADDRESS Lesnaya Ulitsa, 18
METRO Belorusskaya

North

I A Golosov 1927–29

North

I A Golosov 1927–29

Alexandr Nevsky apartments

This multi-sectioned residential complex is situated in an old central district of the city, its immediate environment dominated by picturesque 3- to 9-storey period buildings in diverse styles. Without alluding to history, the softly broken rhythm of the new 6-, 9- and 12-storey blocks successfully imitates that of their more naturally evolved surroundings.

Alexandr Nevskova Ulitsa is set at 13 degrees to the right-angled grid of the nearby streets. Aligning the main façade parallel to the street has resulted in the foreshortening of the building and an enrichment of its articulation, a design approach that was continued into the internal planning. Apartments are of seven different types and have between one and four rooms, their comfortable size being above average for residential units of this period.

The block was a turning point in Meerson's design approach, an expression of his inventive exploration and reworking of the creative possibilities of brick facing to his own satisfaction. The articulation of the façade, the roof line, arches at street level and deep-set balconies all break up the building volume, but in spite of this plasticity and the graded silhouette, the unrelieved monotony of brick can at times convey the impression of a single horizontal mass.

Inventive as always in his approach, Meerson comfortably and in a respectful manner sits this building in its historic surroundings, while at the same time he creates for it a very individual identity.

ADDRESS Alexandr Nevskova Ulitsa
METRO Belorusskaya

A Meerson, E Podolskaya, O Polai, L Vishnichenko 1982–89

North

A Meerson, E Podolskaya, O Polai, L Vishnichenko 1982–89

Intourist garage

Konstantin Melnikov designed several garages, this late example (including workshops and office space) being one of only four that were actually realised. The most interesting aspect of this stunning work is the way in which Melnikov has achieved an impressive dynamic composition with an almost flat five-storey façade. Its vibrancy is developed from a huge round window and a strong diagonal, which gives the impression that the window is rolling down the sloped line (symbolising a ramp). The diagonal junction between the mainly glass surface above and the more solid treatment below does in fact mirror an interior ramp. The window outline is divided by double pilasters which continue across the elevation, while fine mullions establish a cellular glazing pattern in between. At its highest point this window covers the entire five floors of the building.

Below the baseline of the window, running diagonally across the building, the rhythm changes as a combination of solid render and glass creates a more vertical emphasis. Solid pilasters between the narrow windows at this lower level appear as columns turned 45 degrees. Their sharp corners facing the street catch the light and add further depth to the elevation.

To the left a later addition continues the garage façade along the street line, but although rendered in the same light green, it lacks any other qualities found in the original.

ADDRESS Suchshevsky Val, 37
ASSOCIATED ARCHITECT V Kurochkin
METRO Savelovskaya, Rizhskaya

North

K S Melnikov 1934–36

K S Melnikov 1934–36

Soviet Army theatre

Within the restraints of social realism, a desire to create some sort of individual expression led to the extensive use of symbols and emblems in architecture. An extreme example of this can be seen in the design of the Soviet Army theatre, where not only the footprint but the entire volume and spatial organisation of the building are subordinate to the imagery of the five-pointed star.

In this bright, romantic creation of pre-war architecture, the star symbol – or its interpretation as a five-sided form – is repeated throughout, even in the plan of the columns to the colonnade. During construction it became apparent that the impressive symbol was perceivable only in plan so the architects decided to increase the height of the building (already raised on a granite podium) in an effort to create an expressive silhouette – despite the adverse effect this had on the acoustics of the 1500-seat auditorium.

The interior is impressive, with an unprecedented multi-level foyer and a grand main staircase. A huge picture of Stalin used to look down on the stairs but this wall is now discreetly covered.

Organising a functioning theatre within the constraints imposed by the building outline must have been a nightmare; it is not surprising some strange spaces have resulted.

North

ADDRESS Suvorovskaya Ploshchad, 2
METRO Novoslobodskaya, Tsvetnoy Bulvar

K S Alabyan, V H Simbirtsev 1934–40

K S Alabyan, V H Simbirtsev 1934–40

Apartment building

This colourful building near Novoslobodskaya metro station in a historical part of the city centre is first glimpsed from the junction of Dolgorukovskaya Ulitsa. Set back from the busy crossing down a narrow lane, the block maintains a direct visual connection with the main street without revealing its interesting form. An intriguing red and white patterned façade draws one's attention, inviting further investigation.

Using a palette of red brick combined with decorative plaster and natural stone – materials characteristic of many old city buildings – the authors generated a modern plastic façade with a traditional Moscow mood. The fluid volumes, reminiscent of art nouveau, are fully revealed only when one has circled the perimeter and enjoyed the unusual, apparently malleable, forms from all angles. The theme of red and white wave-shaped protrusions and circular columns creates an expressive cheerful image. Also very expressive is the stepped silhouette of the roof, its cool green metal sheeting a reminder of old Russian palaces.

Accommodation within this speculative development is mixed. On the two lower levels, offices share entrance halls situated in a two-storey structure that extends out beyond the residential block above. Between the third and tenth floors are 29 mainly four- and five-roomed apartments, varying from 120 to 200 square metres in area, and a number of duplexes. On the various attic floors are more modest studio apartments. Because of the changing roof line, these are situated on three different levels, with those higher up having access to balconies over lower, flat-roofed areas.

ADDRESS Veskovsky Pereulok, Vladenie 2
ARCHITECTS A Meerson, E Podolskaya, L Vishnichenko
METRO Novoslobodskaya

North

Mosproekt AO (Studio 22) 1995

Mosproekt AO (Studio 22) 1995

North

Durov Theatre

This engaging complex of cylindrical buildings was constructed around a 19th-century gothic building where B V Durov, founder of the theatre, lived and worked from 1908 to 1934. The actors here are of the four-legged variety, their unusual costumed performances a cross between circus and pantomime.

The plan of the building purposely creates a labyrinth of concentric circles, a complexity partially justified by the theatre's multi functions. The compositional centre of the complex is a high round drum housing the 450-seat theatre, its walls richly broken down by oriel windows, balconies, narrow windows and various protrusions. Around the main cylinder, smaller drums provide areas to hold performers of all sizes, from chickens to elephants.

The façade of the main building is ornamented with decorative figures of animals made from sheet copper. Its central focus is a trumpeting elephant calling people to the show. The scale of the sculptures – and indeed of all the buildings – was created with a child's perspective in mind. The original colour scheme was very innovative for its time: the new building, then faced in bright-blue ceramic tiles, was to have contrasted with the gothic building which they meant to render in red, but fortunately this drastic combination never saw the light of day. The present pale-green tiles softly complement the cream stone and rendered elements and blend with the pale-green of the older structure in a homogeneous ensemble.

ADDRESS Durova Ulitsa, 2–4
SCULPTURE D Mitlyansky, V Tyulin
METRO Novoslobodskaya

North

G E Saevich 1974–80

North

G E Saevich 1974–80

Office building conversion

A lively addition to the street in a refreshingly different language is this reconstruction and conversion to office use of a pre-revolutionary textile factory hostel. Working imaginatively with a collage of elements that initially appear arbitrary, the architects have created the building's aesthetic largely in response to practical requirements.

With a talent for unusual renovation and extensions (see Asadov's extension to School No. 20, page 148), they succeeded in doubling the area of the original hostel to 2000 square metres. This increase was achieved by adding two extra floors under a new curved metal roof and placing all vertical communications and services such as air conditioning outside the original building skin. The location of these expressive glass and steel elements has a second practical advantage. The finished structure we see is phase 1 of a two-phase development. Phase 2, a new block which will balance and complete the ensemble, will connect into the existing vertical communication towers.

The entrance was originally planned at ground-floor level, but after underground cables were discovered during excavation it was moved up a floor. Its single steel column, also designed to avoid the cables, umbrellas out to support the open, overhanging roof above. Less successful is the repetition of this dialogue in the design of the suspended entrance bridge.

Internally the design capitalises on the space available in the atrium. Although a relatively modest three-storey space, it has six-storey grandeur, achieved by the wizardry of a mirrored ceiling.

ADDRESS Nizhnaya Krasnoselskaya Ulitsa, 5–6
ENGINEER V Atladze
METRO Krasnoselskaya

North

A P Asadov, A Chastnov 1995

North

A P Asadov, A Chastnov 1995

Burevestnik club

Clubhouses, the most common building type of the 1920s, were relatively small structures, generally located in industrial areas near to where people both lived and worked. Especially active in this genre was Melnikov, who designed six workers' clubs (five within Moscow), all exploring fresh spatial possibilities.

The difficult narrow site allocated for this small clubhouse prompted its unusual solution. On a triangular piece of ground between the street and the main building volume, Melnikov placed an elegant five-petalled glass tower. Protruding from the solid wall and entrance behind are four levels of club rooms, their curved petals of glazing defining the overall appearance of the building. The soft footprint and largely transparent walls underline the contrast between the compact horizontality of the minimalist building and the fluidity of its independent vertical element.

On the second floor of the main building, over the entrance foyer and vestibule, is a 700-seat performance hall with a sports hall immediately behind the stage area. A movable screen between the two areas allows for the possibility of combining them into one larger space. Melnikov had proposed that the floor of the hall open up to reveal a swimming pool below, but this technical innovation never materialised.

North

ADDRESS 3rd Rybinskaya Ulitsa, 17
METRO Sokolniky

K S Melnikov 1929–30

North

K S Melnikov 1929–30

Rusakov club

Each of Melnikov's clubs has its own distinctive character. This clubhouse for public utility workers is his most famous, best known for its memorable form. Unlike the Burevestnik (page 212), this design on an open site was not confined by restrictive boundaries. The bold external volume created is both complex and coherent in expression. Three raked wedges cantilevered over the main entrance clearly describe the volume of the segmented auditoria within. Sculptural in form, this building, in common with much of Melnikov's work, lacks a conventional main façade, revealing instead many different expressions when studied from various angles.

The club's multi-functional design resulted from both a desire to produce new solutions and a shortage of money. Suspended screens hung in front of the balconies divide them from the space below, allowing them to function as separate auditoria. Moving walls divide the auditorium into five spatial elements, each of which could originally have been used separately. The triangular spaces between the wedge-shaped balconies comfortably fit the staircases.

The physical appearance of the building has changed. Windows have been filled in, relief lettering on the sides of the consoles has been removed, the external colour has changed, and the moving screens have disappeared. It has been closed in recent years due to the deterioration of the building fabric; even the external balcony-cum-viewing stand which linked the building with the street is cordoned off because of its appalling state of repair. One hopes the funding will soon be found to reinstate this magnificent example of 20th-century architecture.

North

ADDRESS Stominskaya Ploshchad, 6
METRO Sokolniky

K S Melnikov 1927–29

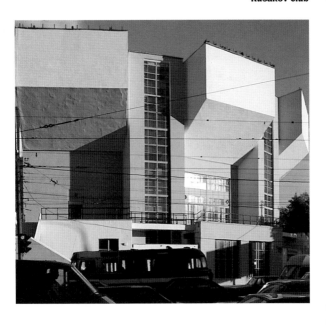

North

K S Melnikov 1927–29

VDNkH

To the north of the city is the VDNKH (now officially called the All Russian Exhibition Centre, VVTS), an amazing place well worth visiting, particularly in the summer. No longer the place of culture, education and propaganda enjoyed by recent generations of Soviets, most of the large halls are now dedicated to trade, crammed with repetitive kiosks, stalls and shops. Despite this commercial intrusion and the destruction of some extraordinary interiors and displays, the park – with its exotic pavilion façades, dramatic sculptural fountains, lake, ponds and other structures – has a festive atmosphere, and one can happily spend a day enjoying this unique record of monumental Soviet architecture saturated with symbols and emblems from the 1930s to the 1950s.

Originally conceived as a temporary exhibition park in 1937, its first event (the All Union Agricultural Exhibition) opened on 1 August 1939. Covering more than 140 hectares, it included more than 250 purpose-built structures, mainly pavilions. The site was heavily landscaped throughout, with trees, flower gardens and glasshouses forming an important part of the huge development.

A general plan prepared in 1937 by V Oltarzhevsky was taken as the basis for this exhibition centre; however, during its construction a government order demanded changes in its architectural character, resulting in serious transformations, including the destruction of almost complete pavilions. Ultimately, the site was organised as a system of sequential, connected squares around which different buildings were grouped. In 1941 the centre was closed, reopening later to exhibit captured German arms.

In 1954 the second period of development began, under architects A Zhukov, R Kliks and others. It included more than 70 new or reconstructed pavilions, with a decorative and eclectic stylisation characteristic

Various architects 1937–80s

Various architects 1937–80s

of post-war Soviet architecture. This stage was barely completed when Communist Party and Government resolutions were passed which radically changed the direction of Soviet architecture. This development therefore marks the official end of social realism or Stalinist classicism.

After 1958, under its new name, The Exhibition of the Economic Achievements of the People's Economy (VDNkH), the expanded development included pavilions entitled 'Machinery Construction', 'Cattle', 'Atomic Energy', 'Radio Electronics' and 'National Education'. The exhibitors proudly demonstrated the achievements of the Soviet Union, with informative displays using models and prototypes. By 1967 additions such as 'Soviet Culture' and 'Geology' had been joined by 'Chemical Industry' and 'Electrification of the USSR'. The most recent addition, on the edge of the park and suitably titled 'National Consumer', is a large-span post-modern hall (by A Bokov, E Budin and others), a virtual shopping centre largely occupied by stalls over two levels.

As you approach the park from the metro, with the curved Cosmos Hotel behind, a wide vista draws you to the main entrance. Designed by L Polyakov as a triumphal arch, it is crowned by G Motovilov's sculptural composition representing a machine worker and a farm girl, both holding a sheaf of wheat.

Opposite the entrance, at the end of a wide avenue punctuated by fountains, is the main Central Pavilion by V Shchuko and V Gelfreikh. This building divides the outer avenue from Kolkhoses (collective farms) Ploshchad, the central space of the whole exhibition. A stepped columned structure, it resembles a wedding cake heavily ornamented with emblems and figurative sculptures, topped with a 35-metre spire. Centred in front of the entrance is P Yatsyno's statue of Lenin, one of the few left standing in the city. Along the perimeter of the avenue are pavilions representing

North

North

Various architects 1937–80s

each of the Soviet republics, with a wide range of colourful architecture and symbolism expressing their diverse cultures. During the Khrushchev era a number of pavilions were destroyed because, according to official aesthetics, they were too decorative.

The Central Pavilion end of Central Square is largely occupied by an octagonal 3700-square-metre granite pond and a lavish gilded-bronze fountain called Friendship of the Peoples (architects K T Topuridze and G D Konstantinovsky; sculptors I M Chaikov, Z V Bazhenova, A I Tenata and Z V Ryleeva). Behind a wall of water-jets are 16 well-proportioned maidens in the national costumes of the former Soviet republics, and at the centre of the composition stands a massive sheaf of wheat. Symbolising abundance and wealth, the sheaf of wheat is used as a decorative element throughout the park, on lamp standards, sculpture and building details. Nine pavilions surround the fountain, their classical treatments representing, to the left, 'Education', 'Biology', 'Physics', 'Chemistry', 'Weights and Measures', and to the right, 'Atomic Energy' and 'Coal Industry' strangely mixed with 'Soviet Press'. Many of the buildings along the avenue connecting the Friendship fountain with the equally stunning Fountain of Stone Flowers at the opposite end are unadorned post-Stalinist replacements. An exception on the right-hand side is the grand former Uzbek Pavilion, in front of which stands an independent lofty pergola on elongated spindly columns. The decoration on and around this attractive star-shaped gazebo is distinctly Asian in origin. The internal hall of the pavilion is presently divided up by freestanding screens and displays of Soviet culture, but in spite of this much of the interesting quality of the original interior is still discernible.

Beyond the animated stone fountain (architect K T Topuridze, sculptor P I Dobrinin) spouting geese, fish and water in all directions, the former

North

Various architects 1937–80s

Various architects 1937–80s

Ukrainian Pavilion by A Tatsy and N Ivanchenko loudly demands attention. A simple, rectangular block, its flat walls are topped with a decorative parapet and the roof crowned with a circular tiara-like spire. The walls are divided in vertical relief and there is abundant applied decoration: glazed ceramic and lattice panels promote the country's rich food supply, a heavy garland of fruit surrounds the massive stained-glass tableau above the main entrance and, as the final seasonings, figurative sculptures (by S M Orlov, Y M Fridman, M I Belostotsky and Z V Ryleeva) stand on the corners of the parapet and at ground level stocky bronze peasants frame the entrance.

Continuing on into Industry Square, one is confronted with the most bizarre sight. A Vostok rocket, once the proud central focus of the square, is suspended above what at first glance appears to be a mechanical scrapyard of defunct planes, but on closer inspection turns out to be an outdoor car showroom occupying the rocket platform and the area between the planes. Behind this spot, especially popular with males of all ages, is the redundant Cosmos Pavilion (designed in 1939 by V Andreyev and I Taranov as the Mechanisation Pavilion). Its massive glazed façade used to reflect the shape of its dynamic vaulted roof, but is now hidden by a dull wall of metal sheeting. In a technically honest expression, the light metal roof resting on monumental supports was originally left open at both ends, but was enclosed and added to in 1954.

Beyond Industry Square the formal layout softens and the greenery increases. One can wander off in several directions, each offering the possibility of further interesting discoveries.

North

ADDRESS Prospekt Mira
METRO VDNkH

Various architects 1937–80s

Various architects 1937–80s

'Worker and Farmer' sculpture

This symbolically rich and romantic creation of Soviet monumental art (part of the USSR Pavilion in Paris in 1937) is a combination of architectural form and visual allegory. The pavilion itself – a long narrow slab-like pedestal on the banks of the river Seine – had an amazing dynamic, stepping up and narrowing into a tower above the entrance. On top, striding heroically forward, were Vera Mukhina's two sculptural figures – a male worker and a female farm worker – hands high in solidarity as they clasped a hammer and sickle. Their clothes rippling out in horizontal pleats echoed the heavy horizontal banding of the stepped cornice.

After the exhibition the monument was returned to Moscow. As a suitable permanent site could not be found, Iofan had to reduce the scale of the original pavilion to fit its present location, at the northern (and at that time main) entrance to the All Union Agricultural Exhibition (see page 216). The resulting low stubby pedestal lacks the grace of the original and is not of a large enough scale for the sculpture; although one can still appreciate the quality of the healthy duo, the balance and dynamism of the original composition have been lost. The figures are constructed in an unusual and clearly visible way, from small rectangular plates of chrome-plated steel.

This sculpture will be familiar to anyone who watches Russian movies, as it is the symbol of Mosfilm. Each film is preceded by an all-round view of the pair, finally focusing on the point where the hammer and sickle appear exactly as on the Soviet flag.

North

ADDRESS Prospekt Mira
METRO VDNKh

B M Iofan 1937

North

B M Iofan 1937

Monument to the Conquerors of Space

On exiting the VDNKH metro station, one's attention is drawn to this dramatic monument to the Soviet conquerors of space. Soaring 100 metres into the sky, this vibrant composition – sculpture/building/obelisk – represents a shining rocket followed by the curved outline of its diverging jetstream faced in sheets of titanium which ignite in reflected sunlight. At its foot the vertical sides of the solid dark granite stylobate are broken by multi-figured reliefs depicting heroic Soviet scientists, engineers and cosmonauts preparing to break new frontiers. On the podium, a sculpted figure (by A P Faidish-Krandievsky) of the founder of cosmonautics, K Tsiolkovsky, seems somewhat stoic and traditional in relation to the rest of the composition.

Along each side of the avenue leading to this monument from Prospekt Mira are bronze busts of cosmonauts and discoverers of space. In 1981 a memorial museum of cosmonautics was opened inside the stylobate.

North

ADDRESS Prospekt Mira
METRO VDNKH

M O Barshch, A N Kolchin 1964

M O Barshch, A N Kolchin 1964

Leningradsky Prospekt

Pravda offices

Panteleimon Golosov, one of the leading architects of constructivism, lived in the shadow of his younger more successful brother Ilya (architect of the Zuev club, page 198), though Panteleimon's contribution to architecture, in teaching and in practice, was equally if not more important.

The offices and printing house of the popular newspaper *Pravda* (truth) are Golosov's masterpiece. A late example of the constructivist approach, they are appreciably larger and more monumental in scale than earlier constructivist works. Composed of two units, a seven-storey editorial building and the lower printing works, their creation was intended as a symbol of the new industrial Russia.

The presence of the building is emphasised by the foreground, which has been opened up by a large landscaped square directly opposite. The office building is simple in form, and close to classicism in its strictly symmetrical planning. Constructivist elements are visible mainly in the treatment of the crisp modern façade. By contrast, the curtain wall suspended from a concrete frame is enlivened at the upper levels. Grey rendered brick walls divide horizontal bands of glazing, while large areas of blank walling conclude the façade either side of the entrance, and large glass panels open up the gable. The façade clearly focuses on the projecting entrance portico with its distinctive curved ends.

The interior, one of the most elegant examples of constructivist architecture, is equally carefully composed.

ADDRESS Pravdy Ulitsa, 24
METRO Savelovskaya

P A Golosov 1930–35

Leningradsky Prospekt

Leningradsky Prospekt

P A Golosov 1930–35

Azhurny apartment building

Burov, regarded as a founder of precast building systems, considered that good architecture could not originate from science or technique alone, but from the skilful application of both. All his work was permeated with this urge to combine art and science. He was convinced too that architecture should be human, linked with nature, descriptive, plastic, tectonic and contemporary. Following this concept through, Burov and Blokhin designed a number of precast buildings with the aim of achieving an expressive method of construction using large-scale repetitive elements. The Azhurny apartment building, the most interesting example of this approach, was the last of this building type by Burov and Blokhin.

The six-storey apartment block, on a corner site between Leningradsky Prospekt and Begovaya Alleya, is innovative and successful in both its planning and composition. The outer walls, a series of vertical panels between pairs of windows, are divided by fine horizontal bands separating the floors, all expressing the building structure. Pairs of non-structural panels screening the kitchen balconies are articulated differently. Designed by the artist Favorsky, these decorative panels work particularly well in screening these intensely utilised, often visually untidy, spaces. In addition, the open concrete lattice with its curved organic ornamentation contrasts well with the rigid structural elements. Practical creativity was also applied to the finish of the building. A dye was added to the concrete before the panels were cast, giving a blue-grey finish that did not require painting. Highlighted against this are the white ornamental details and reinforced-concrete balconies. These decorative elements give the building its name, Azhurny (lace).

ADDRESS Leningradsky Prospekt
METRO Dinamo, Begovaya

Leningradsky Prospekt

A K Burov, B N Blokhin 1939–40

A K Burov, B N Blokhin 1939–40

Begovaya apartment building

This unapologetic apartment block in two tones of grey is situated just off Leningradsky Prospekt. Opening an important city thoroughfare, its length separates a number of residential blocks from the vast open space of a sports complex. The 16-storey, heavy concrete structure has been lifted on to powerful wedge-shaped supports in an effort to relate to the scale of its neighbours and to allow their continued enjoyment of the green space on the far side. Unfortunately, freestanding edifices now shelter under the massive bulk of the building, interrupting the wide clear space created by the unusual squatting legs.

Unique in Moscow, the style of this building comes under the label of neo-brutalism. Like Burov earlier in the building opposite (see page 232), Andrei Meerson has also explored the use of concrete panels, though here the similarity ends. Meerson's plastic and solid expression of the material differs from the prevailing flat panelled façades of most other contemporary apartment blocks.

Internally the building is divided into three groups of apartments accessed from the elevator hall by an internal corridor. Staircases, each encased in an oval concrete shell, protrude along the length of the building, their solid form giving a strong vertical emphasis in contrast to the horizontal lines of the concrete balconies. Everything about this building appears solid, even oversized, down to the concrete balcony guard rails and their supports.

ADDRESS Begovaya Ulitsa, 34–36
METRO Begovaya, Dinamo

A Meerson, E Podolskaya, M Mostovoy, G Klimenko 1965–78

Leningradsky Prospekt

Leningradsky Prospekt

A Meerson, E Podolskaya, M Mostovoy, G Klimenko 1965–78

The Rossiyskaya Finance Academy

Further out of town along Leningradsky Prospekt is a later design by Meerson. Here he continues his exploration of design solutions, this time skirting along the borders of post-modernism.

The Institute of the Sociological Sciences of the Central Committee was commissioned by the Central Committee of the CPSU (Communist Party of the Soviet Union). In the Gorbachev years the complex became a think-tank entitled The Gorbachev Foundation, but after his political demise these activities moved a few doors down to a less high-profile building and The Russian Finance Academy became the principal residents.

A three-storey block with a fort-like entrance on to Leningradsky Prospekt houses study areas and meeting rooms and is connected to the other, higher, blocks by underground passages. Behind, separated by a courtyard, is a nine-storey hostel/hotel block with accommodation for 400 people. Facilities also include a 400-seat hall, a round table discussion room seating 150, recreational facilities, a sports complex, and service areas for teaching and learning.

The exterior walls of light-coloured clay brick combine with concrete details, and curved window heads appear like eyebrows above the windows, their presence highlighted by the use of an unusual red granite render. Dressed in a muted colour scheme, the soft forms and window treatment appear a little dated.

Leningradsky Prospekt

ADDRESS Leningradsky Prospekt, 55
ARCHITECTS T M Bazilevich, G V Baturina, B V Zaionchkovsky, A Meerson, T K Penskaya
STRUCTURAL ENGINEERS O V Kuleshova, A L Nikitin
METRO Sokol, Aeroport

Various architects 1979–89

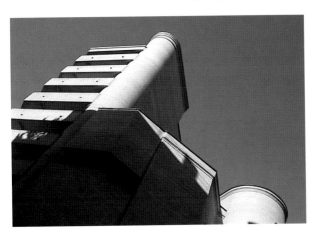

Leningradsky Prospekt

Various architects 1979–89

Sokol Posyelok

In 1918, during a period of post-revolutionary idealism which led to civil war, a group of young architects headed by Ivan Zholtovsky and Alexei Shchusev developed the first master plan for New Moscow. Other members included Konstantin Melnikov, Nikolai Kolli and Ilya Golosov.

The Sokol housing settlement by Nikolai Markovnikov, the first development realised in accordance with the group's layout, is based on the garden-city concept, and consists of detached family units of brick, timber and panels on a 900-square-metre plot. With approximately 45 per cent of the site allocated to green space, tree planting formed an integral part of the original design, with careful consideration given to their shape and colour. The houses were originally intended to be of only two or three standard types, but as the settlement developed the tapestry was enriched, and it became an experiment in low-rise building incorporating different house plans, building styles and materials. Though only 20 minutes from the centre of Moscow, the style of the houses and the layout of the settlement have an atmosphere reminiscent of traditional Russian villages.

This picturesque solution to the problem of housing shortages proved popular in the short term and similar settlements appeared in other cities. However, it soon became clear that this approach could not cope with increasing housing needs, and in addition was incompatible with the developing socialist trend towards communal life. Today, wandering through its streets (all named after Russian artists), one has a feeling of stepping back in time.

ADDRESS Alabyana Ulitsa, Polyenova Ulitsa, Vrubelya Ulitsa, Maly Peschany Pereulok
ASSOCIATED ARCHITECTS A V Shchusev and others
METRO Sokol, CJRJK

N B Markovnikov, V A Vesnin 1923–30

N B Markovnikov, V A Vesnin 1923–30

Private 'kottage' residence

A new class of Russian has arisen from the ashes of Communism – a small but extremely wealthy percentage of the population who demand living accommodation they consider appropriate to their recently acquired life-styles. In addition to new and existing apartment blocks to satisfy these *nouveaux riches* (or 'New Russians' as they are affectionately known), a large number of housing developments and individual houses are springing up around the perimeter of Moscow and beyond.

These individual residences, up to three storeys high, are referred to as 'kottages', though have nothing except their components in common with the modest residences of a similar name. Size and ornament emerge as the most important features of these frequently tasteless pretentious structures; planning control or consideration to siting seem not to have impinged on them.

As with any generalisation there are always exceptions, in this case the restrained Mitino Poselok (Vladilen Krasilnikov's recent housing development) and this individual 'kottage' in the Sokol garden settlement (see page 238). This residence, patently larger than its modest neighbours, occupies a triangular corner site created from two former plots. It was built in two stages: the earlier main house emulates the established rhythm within the settlement in its roof structure and massing, but at the same time has its own modern identity in the fenestration, articulation of the rendered façades and attractive railing details. The extended second phase is a little fussier in detail but detracts little from the overall elegance of this grand home.

ADDRESS Shishkina Ulitsa, 12 (Sokol Posyelok)
METRO Sokol

B E Platonov 1997

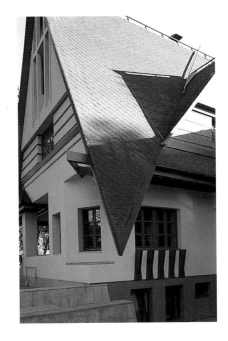

B E Platonov 1997

Leningradsky Prospekt

Northern river terminal

Delicate associations with river vessels provide the imagery for the architecture of this delightful riverside building. Rukhlyadev designed the terminal at a time when the trend was towards traditionalism, using a vocabulary of established elements to create an original ensemble. It stands on the edge of a heavily wooded park which separates the boat station from Leningradskoye Shosse, with only its lofty spire visible from the busy highway.

An elegant two-storey colonnade provides the distinctive architectural aesthetic. Enveloping the length of the building it continues beyond to form semi-circular unroofed enclosures with decorative fountains at both ends. The solid base of the building and its external staircases and ground surfaces are finished in stone, contrasting with the lightness of the elevations. The overall effect relies on the distinction between the horizontality of the building and the vertical tower with its lofty spire.

Formal in its approach, the cubic volume of the coffer-ceilinged main entrance hall is contained by arches separating the adjacent circulation areas to the left and right. Beyond, doors and steps directly opposite the entrance lead down to the river walk and boat terminals below.

Leningradsky Prospekt

ADDRESS Leningradskoye Shosse, 51
ASSOCIATED ARCHITECT V F Krinsky
SCULPTURE I S Yefimov, N Y Danko
METRO Rechnoy Vokzal

A M Rukhlyadev 1932–37

A M Rukhlyadev 1932–37

Lebed micro region

This micro region was developed on the embankment of the Khimki water reserve between a main thoroughfare and a park. Its construction was experimental in that it used brick as a cladding material, exploring fully its artistic possibilities. The achievements of this complex are best appreciated when seen in the context of the surrounding residential developments – badly constructed monotonous precast-panel blocks which accurately represent the typical housing solution of the 1970s and '80s. Following Meerson's initiative here, later constructions were built in the nearby region of Rechnoy Vokzal.

Four 16-storey apartment buildings form part of a multi-functional complex. They appear to be lifted over flat-roofed podiums which join them together in a united group. Turned at an angle above the podiums, the apartment blocks cleverly present solid brick corners to the busy, noisy highway linking Moscow and St Petersburg.

The articulated modelling of the one- and two-storey podiums has lost some of its clarity due to unfortunate 'decorative' signage and other additions which have appeared during the post-Soviet years.

Leningradsky Prospekt

ADDRESS Leningradskoye Shosse, 72–84
METRO Vodny Stadion

A Meerson, E Podolskaya, A V Repety, I Fedorov 1971–76

A Meerson, E Podolskaya, A V Repety, I Fedorov 1971–76

South

Lomonosov State University

A unique city landmark, with its stepped silhouette growing comfortably out of the hill, Lomonosov State University (usually known as MGU) is the largest of Moscow's seven Stalin towers and its first steel-framed building. Situated at a geographic high point on the former Lenin Hills, its distinctive form can be enjoyed from many different parts of the city below. The site for this high-rise structure (and for the other six) was chosen so that the building would serve as a prominent landmark, in this case for those approaching the centre along one of three main highways. On a 16-hectare plot, this most striking architectural representation of social realism stands 75 metres above the Moskva river, with its central 30-storey block rising a further 240 metres.

The 27 main buildings, sports grounds, botanical garden and park make up a harmonious ensemble with an attractive rhythm – from whichever angle it is viewed. In the perfectly symmetrical, ordered composition of the main blocks, four wings rise from 9 to 18 floors to converge on either side of the central skyscraper, which culminates in a 57-metre-high tower and spire.

In front of this powerful stone-clad composition is a large square with fountains and gardens. Leading off it is a long avenue featuring busts of eminent Russian scientists, ending in a viewing platform affording a stunning panorama of the city, with the Lenin Stadium directly below. The picturesque terrace is a popular spot for photographs; on a clear day it is not unusual to see crowds of tourists and wedding parties vying for the best position.

Mathematics and geography are among the 12 faculties occupying the main building, while residential accommodation for both students and teaching staff is located in the wings. From the geological museum on the 28th floor there are wonderful views over the city, but it is best not to

South

L V Rudnev, S E Chernyshev, P V Abrosimov, A F Khryakov 1949–53

South

L V Rudnev, S E Chernyshev, P V Abrosimov, A F Khryakov 1949–53

make it too obvious that you are visiting for this purpose – taking photos from here is strictly forbidden (ask Keith).

In both the exterior and interior, natural stone (including marble, limestone and granite) has been used extensively. There is applied decoration in abundance, as well as sculptures and reliefs awash in Soviet symbols. In front of the main entrance are two sculptures by Vera Mukhina representing a male and female student (see also page 224), and to the rear is a memorial to Mikhail Lomonosov, the famous Russian scholar who founded the university in 1755.

The grandiose scale and sumptuous finishes are also evident in the palatial interiors, which increase in opulence beyond the first floor. Grand marble staircases lead to columned, monumental halls where the ordered decorations and coffered and vaulted ceilings are highlighted by ornamental ceramic and bronze light fittings. This decorative excess culminates in the grand 1500-seat auditorium which is entered off these halls – as are smaller auditoria, lecture halls and lift cores.

It is hard to understand the logic behind the creation of such a lavish environment for study, particularly at a time of great shortages and hardship. But then logic played no part in it – Stalin's wishes were paramount.

South

ADDRESS Vorobyovie Gory, 2
ENGINEER V N Nasonov
METRO Universitet

L V Rudnev, S E Chernyshev, P V Abrosimov, A F Khryakov 1949–53

Palace of Young Pioneers

This large complex for young Soviet pioneers (scouts) on a picturesque green 54-hectare site marked a new direction in Soviet architecture at the beginning of the 1960s. At this time the classical monumentality and architectural rigidity of the Stalinist period was being replaced with modern methods of composition, materials and construction.

In a harmonious ensemble, the blocks are positioned asymmetrically in response to functional requirements. Ignoring alignment with the street below, the long horizontal main building faces on to an extensive square dynamically patterned with criss-crossing stone pathways and interrupted by a 55-metre-high obelisk. To the rear, perpendicular to the ceremonial and entertainment halls, are three parallel structures housing study rooms, studios and other facilities. Protruding towards parkland, their colourful gables are decorated with glazed brick murals. Special attention was given to colour and the synthesis of visual arts both internally and externally. Inventive use was also made of reinforced concrete, most notably in the horizontal band of 'musical' reliefs above the entrance to the concert hall. For the young users of this building, its creators combined architecture, sculpture and paintings within a single environment – something that had not occurred before in Soviet building.

The interior's fluid open-plan layout and winter garden – an airy green space brightly lit from its domed roof – caused quite a sensation in its time and still looks well almost 30 years later.

ADDRESS Kosigina Ulitsa, 17
ARCHITECTS V Yegerev, V S Kubasov, F Novikov, B Paluy, I A Pokrovsky, M Khazhakyan
ENGINEER Y Ionov
METRO Universitet

South

Various architects 1959–62

Various architects 1959–62

Children's Musical Theatre

This theatre near the Palace of Young Pioneers was one of a number of establishments created for children in the newly developed south-west of the city. Also nearby is the circular New Circus (by Y Belopolsky, E Vulykh, S Feoktiskov and V Khavin), built a little earlier in 1971. Originally founded in 1964 by Natalia Sats, People's Artist of the USSR (the highest rank achievable), the remarkable building housing the theatre is clearly for children – even from a distance there is a tangible sense of gaiety in its dynamic form.

The volume of the structure, an almost rectangular mass, is punctured by two intersecting cylinders which rise up above the stone-faced perimeter walls. Abstract and figurative bronze sculptures stand out against the building's buff stone walls; together with those in the grounds they direct one to the various entrances, highlighted by overhanging stone reliefs.

Decorative and colourful, the interior has a relaxed atmosphere, reinforced by bird song drifting through from the aviary. Facilities include a winter garden and a palekh room with walls boldly decorated (mainly in red and black) with fairytale scenes, as found on lacquered palekh boxes. Colour is also cleverly used in the canteen, where a fun shade of blue is further enlivened by a servery area decorated with a bright musical mosaic.

The main theatre, seating more than 1200, has an interesting stepped and scalloped ceiling, and cantilevered rounded balconies.

This musical theatre was the first in the world to be designed specifically for children.

ADDRESS Vernadskovo Prospekt, 5
ENGINEERS A Gorov, C Belov
METRO Universitet

South

A A Velikanov, V D Krasilnikov 1974–79

A A Velikanov, V D Krasilnikov 1974–79

Nagatinskaya Naberezhnaya development

Continuing housing shortages over the decades exerted an impact on vast residential areas. Drab and often monotonous blocks resulted from a need to build as quickly and economically as possible. The seemingly endless repetition of identical rectangular blocks facilitated quick inexpensive prefabrication with maximum standardisation of units.

Set on the banks of the Nagatinskaya flood plain to the south-east of the city, the interesting silhouette and footprint of these three blocks illustrate a more positive approach. At 23 storeys high in the centre, each block steps down and away from the embankment, reducing to 10 storeys at its extremities and creating interesting sculptural forms. The residential buildings were constructed from large precast blue panels, although the colour has dulled somewhat, and the original complementary grey and white colour scheme could do with a lick of paint.

The three blocks of one- to four- room apartments provide a total of 100,000 square metres of accommodation, and comprise a successful compositional solution to high-density planning.

ADDRESS Nagatinskaya Naberezhnaya
ARCHITECTS R P Aldonina, P P Zinovyev, K K Zapasov, B Bergelson, I L Lyutomskaya
ENGINEER B Vilkov
METRO Kolomenskoye

South

Various architects 1972–89

South

Various architects 1972–89

National cancer research centre

This immense building was the first oncology centre to be constructed in the Soviet Union. Located on the edge of a park, its site gently slopes down from the road to the Moskva river below. Rather than the functional architecture of the concrete-panel and stone-faced buildings (typical of the period), it is the planning of this complex facility that is of most interest. Working with the contours of the site, the architects positioned two 600-metre-long blocks in parallel terraces. The first of these, a six-storey building facing the noisier part of the site near the main road, houses facilities involving outside contact: out-patient clinics, reception, and a hotel. The lower building, orientated towards the park, contains mainly service accommodation. Behind the second block and set well back from the street is the curvilinear 22-storey hospital building, its 880 beds distanced from the noise and smell of the traffic.

Passages above ground level link the various buildings, and an underground street with internal transport connects departments and services. Perpendicular to the linear buildings, the passages break up the long winding space between the parallel blocks and create a series of linked external spaces.

ADDRESS Kashirskoye Shosse, 24
ARCHITECTS I M Vinogradsky, V M Orlov, A G Echeistov, E Bekritsky, V K Antonov
METRO Kashirskaya

Various architects 1970s–80s

South

Various architects 1970s–80s

Memorial to the Great Patriotic War

More than 26 million people perished in the Soviet Union during the Second World War, referred to by Soviets as the Great Patriotic War. With such heavy casualties and the incalculable human misery caused, the gigantism and exaggerated pomposity of this complex is perfectly understandable. Positioned on the highest point of Poklonnaya Gora (hill) within the 125-hectare Park Pobedy (victory), this 20-hectare complex – the last Soviet military memorial to be constructed – comprises a museum, sculptural monuments, external exhibition space and a temple.

Dominating the complex and crowned by a massive bronze cupola, a white marble semi-circular colonnade shields the rectangular museum behind. Facing on to the fully circular Victory Square, the building is approached via a wide central path, formally framed by two parallel lines of fountains. Radial walkways named after the defenders of Moscow converge on the centre of the square, marked by a 140-metre-high carved bronze obelisk topped with a statue of Nike, the flying goddess of victory. This sculpture by artist Tsereteli is disparagingly described by Muscovites as 'the grasshopper on the needle'.

To the left of the central path stands a small church dedicated to St George the Victor, patron saint of Moscow. Completed in 1995, it was the realisation of a concept developed in the *perestroika* years of the late 1980s. The result is Georgian in essence, but its architect, Polyansky, was attempting to create a stylised synthesis of the Russian Orthodox Church at the end of the 20th century. It includes a number of elements previously unseen in Russian church architecture – façades decorated with gigantic bronze reliefs, and a day-lit interior.

ADDRESS Kutuzovsky Prospekt
METRO Kutuzovskaya

South

A T Polyansky, V Budiev, L V Vavakin and others 1983–95

South

A T Polyansky, V Budiev, L V Vavakin and others 1983–95

Leninsky Prospekt

Atrium restaurant

When opened in 1989, this extraordinary little restaurant made an enormous impression. It broke new ground on many fronts, being the first restaurant to be built and run by a cooperative, as well as the first project to be realised by a talented prize-winning team who had previously been recognised only as 'paper architects'. Furthermore, it was in a style hitherto unseen in Soviet interiors.

Practically hidden beneath an innocuous multi-storey Soviet apartment building, the restaurant's modest, if incongruous, entrance portico is easy to miss. On venturing from the dull street into the flamboyant theatrical interior one is wowed by the Mediterranean courtyard-like dining hall decorated with motifs adapted from late Roman and Byzantine architecture. The mannerist, slightly distorted classical forms are consistent with the graphic work of both Alexander Brodsky and Ilya Utkin.

In order to realise their design, the architects took on the role of builders, and actually crafted the entire interior themselves. Applying style, a touch of irony and much fantasy, the architects/masons/builders (as in medieval times) spent months painting and carving the imaginative plaster shapes.

Leninsky Prospekt

ADDRESS Leninsky Prospekt, 44
METRO Leninsky Prospekt

A Brodsky, I Utkin, E Monakhov 1988

A Brodsky, I Utkin, E Monakhov 1988

VTsSPS

Construction on this finely adorned trade-union building, unique in its imagery and style, started before the war and was completed only towards the end of the 1950s. By this time there had been a sharp move away from the decorative excesses of Stalinist classicism. Unnecessary and superfluous additions were now out of favour, and this is probably why some of the original ideas were never implemented.

The zigzag plan of this public building is said to echo the ideas of the constructivist period. Architectural forms in the composition have been drawn from two sources: the Italian Renaissance and the art of Pompeii. A large coffered cornice overhangs at roof level, exaggerated by the orchestrated use of a diminishing perspective. The walls of the projecting corners depict motifs from Pompeii. Sometimes these creations seem to step out from the wall to become architectural forms, such as the canopies on the balconies. In contrast, corner towers with arched loggias on the upper levels have a more solid expression.

Architectural ornamental devices are handled confidently in a modern interpretation of the classics, with elements such as *trompe-l'oeil* borrowed from the theatre. The resulting aesthetic of this unusual building could be labelled post modern.

Leninsky Prospekt

ADDRESS Leninsky Prospekt, 42
METRO Leninsky Prospekt

A V Vlasov 1936–59

A V Vlasov 1936–59

Sberbank of Russia

On a corner to the east of Leninsky Prospekt two narrow glazed towers – one 26 storeys high, the other 16 – dominate the surrounding area. Both grow from a massive base of two four-storey rectangular blocks. Aligned to the bordering streets, the repetitive vertical rhythm of their jade-green glass and stone façade is reminiscent of 1970s architecture. The most interesting aspect of the building design is an open rotunda leading to the building entrance from the prospekt. Faced in green serpentine stone, this ceremonial circle brings an element of the unexpected to the otherwise slightly monotonous canvas of this 85,000-square-metre savings bank headquarters.

In a logically planned interior, working and administrative zones (offices, banking floor and 600-seat conference hall) are separated from service and recreational areas (canteen, sports and health centres), yet connected by passages. The two basement levels include parking for 350 cars, a bank store and technical areas.

Unlikely to be accessible unless you have savings in the mega-rouble category is the sophisticated interior of the presidential section by Sergei Skuratev. In a limited palette of glass, corporate stainless steel, wood and white plaster, the crisply detailed design has a pleasant balance. Warm wooden floors and panelling complement beautifully articulated glazed screens and doors in polished stainless steel. Curved lines in the wall of the president's study and the corridor ceiling contrast with the geometric squares and horizontal lines of the main design pattern.

ADDRESS Vavilova Ulitsa, 21
ARCHITECTS V Steyskal, N Lutomsky (Russia); H Hoos, D Wonderlich-Buis (Germany)
METRO Leninsky Prospekt

Various architects 1996

Leninsky Prospekt

Various architects 1996

Presidium of the USSR Academy of Sciences

Sited on a level plateau 30 metres above the Moskva river, this building with its roof dominating the city skyline is unmissable. Crowning an 18-storey white stone-faced block are two golden rectangles, each several storeys high and composed of a filigree pattern of open cubes. Incredibly, these huge volumes are empty voids, their only purpose apparently is to attract attention, a function they perform admirably.

The practical development of the brief for this novel building type spanned some 30 years of construction and reconstruction. Although designed as a multi-functional complex for the governing body of the Academy of Sciences, the complex is now mainly occupied by offices.

On a large podium, a later courtyard composition exhibits a range of animated designs. Continuity, both within its different parts and with the earlier blocks, is maintained solely by the exotic palette of white and gold and the use of squares – in the module for the gold glazing bars dividing the gold-tinted glass, in the larger module of gold panels, in relief patterns on the white stone panels, and in the shape of many of the bevelled windows. Whatever one thinks of the resulting flamboyance, it is clear that the architects enjoyed themselves in the process.

On the slopes below this 4.6-hectare site is the Andreevsky Monastery, established in the 16th century, whose location, character and composition are claimed to have influenced this scheme.

ADDRESS Kosygina Ulitsa, 32a
METRO Leninsky Prospekt

Leninsky Prospekt

Y Platonov, A Batyreva, E Zakharov, A Zvezdin 1960s–90s

Leninsky Prospekt

Y Platonov, A Batyreva, E Zakharov, A Zvezdin 1960s–90s

Kaluga Gate buildings

The north-east part of the former Kaluzhskaya Ploshchad is enclosed by two crescent-shaped eight-storey residential blocks culminating in tall corner gate towers. Completed by the Leningrad architects Levinson and Fomin in 1939, the buildings and square were designed as gates into the city. Only the right-hand block was realised before the Second World War and it is interesting to compare this with the later building on the left, a monumental ensemble characteristic of socialist realism, with additional decoration and ordered elements typical of the post-war years. On these luxury apartments for the Soviet elite – as on many other developments – prisoners formed a large part of the workforce. On this particular site they included the interned writer Alexander Solzhenitsyn. It is quite likely that his work here included laying floors – a character in his novel *The First Circle* laid parquet floors in this building.

In the 1950s development spread towards the south-west of Moscow, including Leninsky Prospekt. At 41 kilometres long, it remains one of the city's main arteries and its longest avenue.

In the 1960s the south side of the square was developed. Separated from the main square by a railway bridge, this part is now called Ploshchad Gagarina. In its centre on a 30-metre-high column is a 13-metre high sculpture commemorating Yuri Gagarin, the first cosmonaut in space. This futuristic piece in titanium was designed in 1980 by Y Belopolsky, P Bondarenko and F Gazhevsky.

ADDRESS Leninsky Prospekt, 30–37
METRO Leninsky Prospekt

E A Levinson, I I Fomin, A E Arkin 1939–50

Leninsky Prospekt

E A Levinson, I I Fomin, A E Arkin 1939–50

Communal student housing

This very elegant narrow constructivist building was strongly influenced by Le Corbusier, and its volumetric spatial composition is one of the best of its time. In the early days of the Soviet state, this experimental residential building type – which encouraged communal activities – was expected to have a big future. Incredibly, the skinny 200-metre-long eight-storey building included sleeping facilities for 2000 students. Each individual was allocated a mere 6 square metres in one of 1000 two-person railway carriage-like 'sleeping cabins'. Dressing and all other activities were carried out in various communal areas.

In a separate three-storey block are grouped the entrance vestibule, canteen, and study halls, naturally lit with rooflights. Both this and the sleeping block are connected to a sanitary block where students could shower and change.

The interiors of the building are stamped with a clean geometry, especially striking in the Le Corbusier-influenced internal ramp connecting the floors. A continuous row of narrow horizontal windows creates an unusual impression internally. It is obvious that great attention was paid to the details of the interior, many of which remain intact and are still visible today, though the layout of the building was changed after the Second World War.

ADDRESS Ordzhonikidze Ulitsa, 8–9
METRO Leninsky Prospekt

I S Nikolaev 1929–30

I S Nikolaev 1929–30

Shabolovka communal house

In the mid 1920s, in response to the rapidly growing population and increasing housing needs, a number of specific areas were allocated for residential development, their locations determined by developing industrial zones. Though positioned in close proximity to the factories, the apartment blocks housed people from all walks of life. Developed intensively over a short period of time, these districts are worth wandering through, as they are rich in interesting examples of constructivism.

The Shabolovka communal house, the result of a competition in 1925, is situated directly across the road from the Shabolovka residential district. Intended to combine traditional types of apartments with a communal lifestyle, it was criticised for an insufficient differentiation of functions. Nevertheless, this interesting experiment with its stepped U-shaped footprint, rendered façade, and light cantilevered balconies is exceptional for its rationality and simplicity.

The neighbouring housing scheme, the result of a friendly competition within the progressive group of architects known as ASNOVA, was designed by Nikolai Travin and others between 1927 and 1929. In an original spatial arrangement, five- and seven-storey buildings occupying an entire city block are laid out in an L-shape at 45 degrees to the surrounding streets. The zigzag pattern of the residential blocks creates striking perspectives and intimate yards in between the blocks.

ADDRESS Lesteva Ulitsa, 18
METRO Shabolovskaya

Leninsky Prospekt

G Volfenzon, S Azhikovich, E Volkov 1926–27

Leninsky Prospekt

G Volfenzon, S Azhikovich, E Volkov 1926–27

Radio tower

This 140-metre-high steel radio tower was the first large post-revolutionary structure – and as such became an important symbol for a short period of radical romanticism during which great innovation and experimentation were encouraged.

The imagery expressed by engineer Vladimir Shukhov in this elegant rational structure has been associated with Vladimir Tatlin's vision for the monument to the Third International in 1919/20.

Originally the tower was designed to be 350 metres high; however, it ended up considerably lower, not for structural reasons but due to a lack of finance. Even at its reduced height, the complex structure towered over the neighbouring buildings, allowing Moscow radio to broadcast world wide. When built, the tapering structure consisted of five diminishing hyperboloids rather than the nine that had been planned. Shukhov created this delicate lattice structure with a curvilinear web-like silhouette using straight steel bars. The method used to erect it was also original: the tower was raised using Shukhov's own telescopic method of assembly, which required no scaffolding.

Shukhov was responsible for many and varied structures throughout Russia, both before and after the revolution.

Leninsky Prospekt

ADDRESS Shabolovskaya Ulitsa, 53
METRO Shabolovskaya

V G Shukhov 1919–22

V G Shukhov 1919–22

Park Place

In this multi-functional complex, three blocks of between seven and 24 storeys in height are united over a two-storey podium with a central atrium. As well as short-stay serviced apartments and offices for business people, the complex includes public, social and administrative areas, an underground garage and a children's playground with sports complex above. The 333 apartments (including some duplexes) can be entered either directly from the street or through the public atrium.

The sculptural massing of the blocks is unusual for Moscow and is very attractive, though it does not stand up to close inspection – the white paint on the concrete façades is already starting to peel and looks a bit tatty. Vertical circulation is expressed as curved elements at the end of each block, contrasting pleasantly with the horizontal emphasis of the windows and balconies. Not following a rigid pattern, the juxtapositioning of the recessed balconies and overhangs creates an interesting rhythm.

Across the corner, set back diagonally between two blocks, the main entrance is clearly identified by a solid arch, but is disappointing in its tendency to post-modernism.

ADDRESS Leninsky Prospekt, 113
ENGINEERS B S Mesburg, G S Vainstein
METRO Yugo-Zapadnaya

Y Belopolsky, N Lyoutomsky, Youksel Erdimir (Turkey) 1992

Leninsky Prospekt

Y Belopolsky, N Lyoutomsky, Youksel Erdimir (Turkey) 1992

Moscow Metro System

Introduction

Moscow's metro system, one of the proudest achievements of the Soviet era, includes some of the most spectacular examples of subterranean architecture in the world. Commissioned in 1935, the first line of the 'Moscow Metropolitan in the name of Lenin' was completed in 1938, becoming the most popular architectural complex of the decade. While each station was to have its own identity, all stations on a particular line were to possess a certain common element. Each underground station had also to be tangibly linked – by topical or material associations – with its entrance above ground. After the initial successful achievements, this approach was continued in later developments.

In the underground halls the architects and engineers accomplished their aspiration to remove the sensation of being buried deep underground. Travelling on the metro one experiences none of the psychological stress usually associated with being underground, though the often unbelievably long escalators can be a bit hair-raising when operating at full speed during rush hours.

As the network continued to develop, it became the chief means of efficiently transporting millions of passengers throughout the city every day, and it remains a major part of the city's infrastructure. As a reflection of architectural trends, the stations are a unique historical record of the last 60 years. Fortunately the main spaces have remained free of advertisements, though they have intruded into the train carriages and on to the walls of the escalators, together with indecipherable promotional recordings which assault the ears of uninterested passengers.

Choosing a small sample from more than 150 stations is difficult, as those of interest could fill an entire volume. The following attractive features from a few of the stations not included here are worth a particular mention: the stained-glass panels on the columns of Noboslobodskaya;

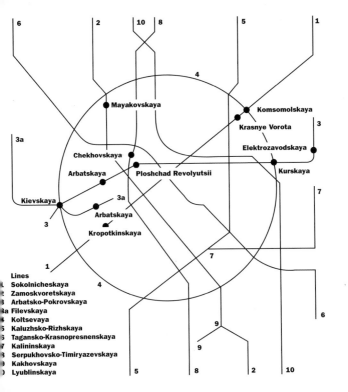

Lines
1. Sokolnicheskaya
2. Zamoskvoretskaya
3. Arbatsko-Pokrovskaya
3a. Filevskaya
4. Koltsevaya
5. Kaluzhsko-Rizhskaya
6. Tagansko-Krasnopresnenskaya
7. Kalininskaya
8. Serpukhovsko-Timiryazevskaya
9. Kakhovskaya
0. Lyublinskaya

the narrow freestanding uplighters in the centre of Semenovskaya; the solid working figures between ribbed supports in Baumanskaya; the stepped marble surround to arches and niches together with zigzag light fittings in Dobrininskaya; the dynamic curved criss-cross patterns on the ceiling of the single-tunnelled central-platformed Aeroport; the elegant curves of the unusual oval vaults between central supports at Sokol; and the high soft curves of Pavelskaya's ceiling where diverging lines springing from Soviet motifs shield uplighters positioned on top of slender marbled columns.

Kropotkinskaya

Notable for its restrained and elegant design, the underground hall to this station was constructed in the first stages of the development of the metro. Originally, Alexei Dushkin and Yakov Likhtenberg's proposal was neo-classical in approach, its theatrical pomposity reflecting the proximity of the intended Palace of Soviets (on which site now stands the reinstated Christ the Saviour cathedral).

The realised design could not have been more different in its originality and restraint. Elegant structural supports constitute the single decorative element, with soft uplighting emphasising their sculptural forms. Hexagonal in outline and faced in pale-grey marble, the columns mushroom out towards the top to conceal the recessed lighting. A soft even luminescence throughout the hall creates the impression of a floating ceiling. The floor to the combined platforms and hall is finished in grey and pink granite slabs, with the platform walls also dressed in two-tone marble.

There are two exits from this station, one on to Volkhonka Ulitsa near the cathedral and the other on to Kropotkinskaya Ploshchad, via an over-ground vestibule. This small traditional structure consists of two covered staircases. These buildings continue into retail units behind and are linked by a raised coffered arch framing the start of Gogolevsky Bulvar.

Moscow Metro System

METRO LINE Sokolnicheskaya

A N Dushkin, Y G Likhtenberg 1935

Moscow Metro System

A N Dushkin, Y G Likhtenberg 1935

Krasnye Vorota station vestibule

Considered one of the best-realised examples of constructivism, the above-ground vestibule to Krasnye Vorota (Red Gates) station contrasts greatly with the station below (see page 292).

Situated on the border of the Sokolnichesky and Baumansky districts, the freestanding pavilion has the shape of a portal shell, bringing to mind an old-fashioned radio set. Stepping back in concentric semi-circular ribs of concrete, the shape of the façade is highlighted by the contrasting strips of red marble which separate the structures. Though small in size, the vestibule's colour and unusual form generate a strong presence among its multi-storey neighbours. The axis of the pavilion has been laid exactly in line with that of the triumphal gates that previously stood on the site and which give the station its name. The gates were constructed at the beginning of the 18th century to commemorate victory over the Swedes. Later they became known as Krasnye Selo because a road passed under the gates to the village of Krasnye.

The red marble used in this station is said to have come from the original Christ the Saviour cathedral after its demolition in 1932.

Moscow Metro System

ADDRESS Krasnye Vorota Ploshchad
METRO Krasnye Vorota

N A Ladovsky 1935

Krasnye Vorota

Entered from either the shell-like pavilion (page 290) or from a second entrance in the basement of the socialist-realist-style Lermontov Tower (page 162), the neo-classical style of Ivan Fomin's underground hall relates more closely to the latter. Lying deep underground, this station became a prototype, with many other stations following the design principles established here.

The central hall is divided from the platform by wide concrete supports; these have been visually reduced in scale by recessed arched centres which are dressed in a lighter coloured stone, and so stand out against a background of red marble. A cornice separates these powerful pylons from the alternating rows of squares and pentagons which form the pattern of the curved white coffered ceiling. The rich warm colours of the columns, faced in three different marbles, contrast with the golden tones of the platform walls behind.

Moscow Metro System

METRO LINE Sokolnicheskaya

I A Fomin 1935

I A Fomin 1935

Mayakovskaya

The elegant simplicity of this light silvery underground hall, constructed as part of Moscow's second metro line, is a pleasant contrast to the established rich decorative neo-classical style of the period. A full-scale spatial model of the hall won its author Alexei Dushkin the grand prize at the World Fair in New York.

Construction of this remarkable underground hall in one of the deepest stations was unique. The massive supports which usually separate the platforms from the central hall were replaced by thin metal columns clad in rippled stainless steel. For the first 2 metres their corners were faced with small bands of Ural stone.

A clear elegant curved section, the roof is highlighted by the profiled polished metal which continues from the columns across the ceiling to form ribbed arches along the length of the hall. Between each arch the ceiling is raised even higher, with decorative ventilation grilles and uplighters leading one's gaze towards the colourful mosaic panels in oval cupolas. The images in artist A Deyneka's panels all follow the same theme: the Soviet sky over 24 hours. Slabs of white marble form rectangular patterns in the floor, divided by strips of grey and pink granite.

There are two exits from the station; the main one brings you out opposite a monument to the Soviet poet Vladimir Mayakovsky, erected in 1958 in the centre of the square named in his honour.

Mayakovskaya station was closed during the Second World War in order to serve as an air-raid shelter. On 6 November 1941 Stalin held a sombre meeting here to mark the anniversary of the October revolution. The venue was chosen because the Germans were at this time closing in on the bombed city.

METRO LINE Zamoskvoretskaya

A N Dushkin 1936

A N Dushkin 1936

Ploshchad Revolutsii

Waiting on the platform of this station, together with the numerous cast-bronze figures crouched under the arches, one experiences a comfortable feeling of companionship. One also feels protected by these larger-than-life revolutionaries – sailors, soldiers, airmen and farmers – all waiting attentively with their various weapons at the ready. Created in Leningrad by sculptor M Manizer, this gallery of Soviet figures was intended to depict the power and strength of the young state, in both its current achievements and its great past.

Resting on plinths of black Armenian marble, the arches and figures are framed in plain bands of red marble, while the floor below is a simple checkerboard pattern of grey stone. Above this warm palette of colours, criss-crossing lines etched in to the arched plaster ceiling form a light yet dynamic pattern, highlighted by two rows of simple pendant lights. While not competing for attention with the dramatic elements below, they are a pleasant relief on an otherwise plain white surface.

This sociable station by the talented Dushkin is decorated with all the pomp and circumstance of the time, unlike his more restrained designs at Kropotkinskaya and Mayakovskaya.

In the centre of the hall, stairs lead down to a crossing to the adjoining Theatralnaya and Okhotny Ryad. At the ends of the hall two sets of escalators take passengers up to Ploshchad Revolutsii and Nikolskaya Ulitsa.

Moscow Metro System

METRO LINE Arbatsko-Pokrovskaya

A N Dushkin 1936–38

Moscow Metro System

A N Dushkin 1936–38

Elektrozavodskaya

The stunning ceiling of this underground hall rests on two rows of pylons, each decorated with marble relief. Completed before the end of the Second World War, the reliefs represent the continuing war effort of the Soviet people. These pale pictorial panels illustrating the people at work in industry, agriculture and transport during the war years are highlighted by the contrasting facing of red Georgian marble on the platform walls behind. Another attractive feature on the wide columns are the ventilation ducts covered in open lattice-work bronze grilles. The floor is paved in black and grey slabs framed in pink/yellow Crimean marble.

One is not at first aware of these and other interesting elements, as it is the curved circular patterned ceiling that grabs one's immediate and full attention. This amazing bright curved roof consists of about 300 cupola impressions, each holding electric lamps in a fine promotion of the nearby electrical factory after which the station is named.

There is one exit from the station on to Bolshaya Semenovkaya Ulitsa through a ground-level six-cornered building. At the entrance to the pavilion there is a pleasant group sculpture representing the metro construction workers. On the walls of the escalator and the red marble-faced ticket hall are medallion portraits of famous scientists.

Other stations by Igor Rozhin are Park Kultury on the circle line, completed in 1950, and the elegant Smolenskaya on the same line as this station, completed in 1953.

METRO LINE Arbatsko-Pokrovskaya

V G and I E Rozhin 1944

Kurskaya

The 1950s saw a trend towards the use of applied architectural and representative art in the decoration of interiors; this was particularly popular in the design of metro stations. One of the outstanding stations of this period is Kurskaya, in the design of both the underground hall servicing the circle line and the circular hall above linking the three adjoining stations. The lightness and festive atmosphere of this station have been achieved by the use of progressive engineering methods and a restricted palette of finishes.

Unlike many post-war stations, Kurskaya is not overloaded with heroic details. Modestly, the underground hall is faced in white marble. Dividing the simple curved ceiling from the fluted columns below is a horizontal cornice relief, its gilded metal garlands representing the blossoming of the motherland. Golden metal grilles and suspended light fittings provide the only other decoration. In the centre of the hall connecting staircases between powerful supports are emphasised by a change in the ceiling treatment.

Continuing up by escalator, one arrives in the elaborate underground hall and circular vestibule. Surrounded by marble columns, this dynamic space is dominated by a broad central column. Above a gilded ornate capital its decorative surface sprouts out, shielding light sources before merging into the ceiling. Unfortunately this interesting space is somewhat spoiled by the recent intrusion of offensive kiosks.

Moscow Metro System

METRO LINE Koltsevaya

G Zakharov, Z Chernysheva 1949

Moscow Metro System

G Zakharov, Z Chernysheva 1949

Komsomolskaya

Unusually spacious for a deep-set hall, this unbelievable station was part of the metro's fourth phase. Begun during the last years of the Second World War (but not completed until 1952), this sumptuous palace exudes an heroic, triumphal mood. Passing through the monumental lower hall one feels unsuitably dressed, especially when wrapped up against the elements. It would be far more appropriate to glide through these marbled halls to the strains of Rachmaninov, swathed in rustling silk.

A structure developed especially for this project resulted in a central hall almost double the height of those at other stations. Its striking vaulted ceiling is characteristic of the post-war period and saturated in the pathos of victory. Within huge hexagons and triangles formed by raised plaster-work, massive bronze chandeliers highlight colourful mosaics, their victorious images framed by baroque cartouches.

Supported by two rows of 68 columns, the 10-metre-high vaulted ceiling of this grandiose hall spans 190 metres. Eight ceiling panels by P Korin depict the victory of the Russian people and their struggle for independence. Six of the panels depict military leaders and their armies, including Soviet soldiers and officers at the walls of the fallen Reichstag. A panel depicting Beria and Stalin in Red Square was changed after their demise, and a later addition, Khrushchev, was removed in 1964.

This stop services three of the city's main railway stations, all situated on Komsomolskaya, the capital's busiest square.

A less elaborate earlier station on the Kirovsko-Frunskaya line was constructed in 1935 by D N Chechulin. It has a high-ceilinged under-ground hall supported by two rows of golden marble-faced columns. Decoration includes majolica plates depicting young Komsomol workers.

METRO LINE Koltsevaya

A V Shchusev, V Kokorin, A Zabolotnaya 1952

A V Shchusev, V Kokorin, A Zabolotnaya 1952

Arbatskaya

There are two stations called Arbatskaya, with an extensive system of underground halls and corridors running from Vozdvizhenka Ulitsa to Arbatskaya Ploshchad. It is easy to become confused in these stations as there are also passageways to the adjoining Lenin Library, Alexandrovsky Sad, and Borovitskaya.

The earlier station, built in 1935 by architect L Tellitsky, exits on to Arbatskaya Ploshchad from a freestanding over-ground pavilion. This tiered, rectangular structure with red-rendered façades has an interesting form resulting from its curved surrounding canopy and the cylindrical crown which tops the building and reflects the circular plan of the steps below.

In contrast to the rectangular high columned space of this shallow underground hall, the later station is situated at a deeper level and has a dramatic engulfing shape. Arching upwards from low marbled plinths, double rope-edged beams emphasise the section of the vaulted vestibule. Completing the decoration are ceramic bouquets of flowers and a double row of massive ecclesiastical bronze chandeliers. A mural of Stalin at the top of the escalator, although now painted over, can still be made out on close inspection.

Moscow Metro System

METRO LINE Filevskaya

L Polyakov, V Pelevin 1953

L Polyakov, V Pelevin 1953

Kievskaya

The central part of Kievskaya's main underground hall (by E Katonin, V Skugarev and G Golubov) has an elegant snow-white vaulted ceiling, connected to the platforms by parabolic arches framed with ropes of plasterwork characteristic of 17th-century Ukrainian architecture. Marble-faced walls, rich plaster ornament, and golden chandeliers give the station a celebratory atmosphere. There are also decorative mosaic panels by Ukrainian artist A Mizin, in which he diplomatically intended the tableaux to reflect a theme of friendship between the Ukrainian and Russian peoples.

The station on the circular line by L Lilye, V Litvinov, M Markovsky and V Dobrokovsky opened a year earlier in 1953. Its vestibules and main halls differ from those of the later station in their use of ethnic decoration, such as the columns faced in white Ural marble, crowned by a complex ceramic cornice with Ukrainian folk motifs. The vaulted ceiling decorated with huge plasterwork medallions is yet again on the theme of working people, this time in the Soviet Ukraine. On the end wall of the hall is a bright mosaic depicting workers on holiday in Kiev. The far platform walls in white and grey marble have floors of grey granite slabs.

There are two exits, via a system of underground passages which also link up with other stations. It is worth paying attention to the overground escalator hall where tall round marble columns support a wide cornice screening the light fittings. Light reflected off the spherical ceiling makes the whole hall appear bright and spacious. Ornate chandeliers supplement the main lighting and add to the richness of the decoration.

METRO LINE Koltsevaya

Various architects 1953, 1954

Various architects 1953, 1954

Chkalovskaya

This is one of a number of recent metro stations on a line opened in 1996. As with earlier constructions, each of the new stations has a vestibule/ticket area below ground, or a building at ground level with escalators connecting it to the lower hall and train platforms.

The brief for each station stipulated that it include a work of art. In this station it takes the form of a circular metal cage-like construction suspended from the ceiling of the upper vestibule. Together with similar freestanding wall screens, it evokes an atmosphere reminiscent of the New York subway.

More successful is the clear arched form of the lower hall. One's gaze is drawn to the ceiling, where elegant and slender integrated light fittings appear as curved ribs between the white fibrous-cement panels which carry the ceiling into the columned walls. Here the tube lights terminate in recesses cut into the stone.

A series of concentric squares down the centre of the hall floor contrasts with and emphasises the curves of the ceiling and the soft curved arches of the passages to the platforms. Described as umbrellas, these curved ceiling panels allow ground water to run down their outer skin and drain through the columns on either side.

Clean and elegant, the lines of this station are evocative of Dushkin's Mayakovskaya, interrupted only by signage across the ribbed rows of ceiling lights and plaster.

METRO LINE Stroyashchiesya/Lyublinskaya

Metro Gitro Transport: N Alyoshina, L Gonchar, L Pavlov 1996

Moscow Metro System

Metro Gitro Transport: N Alyoshina, L Gonchar, L Pavlov 1996

Index

Moscow: a guide to Soviet and post-Soviet architecture

Moscow: a guide to Soviet and post-Soviet architecture

Moscow: a guide to Soviet and post-Soviet architecture

Moscow: a guide to Soviet and post-Soviet architecture